BITCOIN PIZZA

BITCOIN PIZZA

THE NO-BULLSHIT GUIDE TO BLOCKCHAIN

SAMANTHA RADOCCHIA

LIONCREST
PUBLISHING

BITCOIN PIZZA
The No-Bullshit Guide to Blockchain

ISBN   978-1-5445-0443-8 *Hardcover*
        978-1-5445-0441-4 *Paperback*
        978-1-5445-0442-1 *Ebook*

CONTENTS

INTRODUCTION 11

PART I: BLOCKCHAIN AND BITCOIN: THE CHICKEN AND THE EGG

1. A DAY IN THE LIFE JUST AROUND THE CORNER 33
2. THE MYSTERIOUS SATOSHI NAKAMOTO...53
3. BLOCKCHAIN: MUCH MORE THAN BITCOIN'S BACKBONE...........................69
4. BLOCKCHAIN: DECENTRALIZATION, GOVERNANCE, AND COMMUNITY BUILDING 95
5. BUILDING THE TRUSTLESS ECONOMY 113

PART II: CRYPTOCURRENCY AND CRYPTOGRAPHY

6. IT'S ALL IN THE GAME..133
7. THE ZILLION-DOLLAR PIZZA: BITCOIN'S MYTHOLOGY AND EVOLVING VALUE(S).....149
8. TOKENS: CRYPTOCURRENCY BEYOND BITCOIN 173
9. NO-COINERS AND CRYPTO-SKEPTICS...199

PART III: BLOCKCHAIN: THE LINKS ARE SPREADING!

10. PARTY LIKE IT'S 1994!...229
11. DEMAND CHAINS: A NEW, BLOCKCHAIN-ENABLED WAY OF DOING BUSINESS........249
12. UNLOCKING BIG DATA: BETTER CALL BLOCKCHAIN! 271
13. RETROFITTING: SECURE COLLABORATION AMONG COMPETITORS......................295
14. BUILDING A BLOCKCHAIN-BASED CULTURE 317

CONCLUSION 337
ACKNOWLEDGMENTS...349
ABOUT THE AUTHOR 355

The world as we have created it is a process of our thinking. It cannot be changed without changing our thinking.

ALBERT EINSTEIN

INTRODUCTION

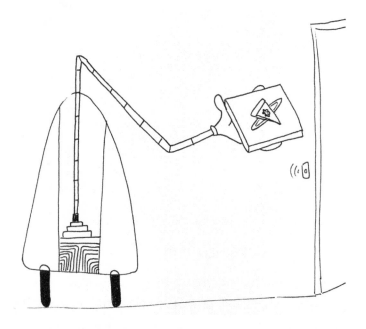

If you're thinking to yourself, "I came here for the Pizza," fear not! I assure you you'll get it, most likely from one of those automated robot Pizza delivery services that are all the rage these days. Don't believe me? They do exist.

Domino's is leading the charge with on-demand Pizza production and delivery. Zume Pizza has raised hundreds of millions to automate the Pizza production and delivery process using robotics and AI. Soon, your Pizza will be made on demand in the back of an autonomous vehicle routed directly to you upon order.[1]

But that's beside the point. Or is it?

MAPQUEST VERSUS GOOGLE MAPS

How many of you out there have ever used a ride-sharing application like Uber or Lyft? How about home-sharing, like Airbnb? How about food delivery? For the bravest of us, how about electric scooters or bikes on demand? If I

---

1   Melia Robinson, "This Startup Is Raising $750 Million to Outmaneuver Domino's and Pizza Hut with Pizzas Made by Robots—Check It Out," *Business Insider*, August 19, 2018, https://www.businessinsider.com/zume-pizza-robot-expansion-2017-6.

were to guess, I would say 85 percent of you, maybe more. Welcome to the mass tech-adoption market!

What you may not know is that many of these businesses began running their services with the Google Maps location services API (application programming interface). Why is this important? Just think: in the late nineties and early 2000s, MapQuest was queen. You could go to its website, enter two locations, and get directions. You printed them out, referred to them while driving, then stuffed them into your glove compartment, adding to the accumulating mess.

Fast-forward to 2005. Google Maps, a similar mapping and directions tool, entered the market. Yet it was different. It wasn't just a better map. It launched its API, which allowed other developers to use and build on top of its data. Within a few years, we saw the rise of the demand economy. We saw Uber. We saw Lyft. In short order, we saw the various offshoots: "Uber for food delivery," "Uber for dog walking," "Uber for companionship," "Uber for doctors on demand," "Uber for _____." You fill in the blank.

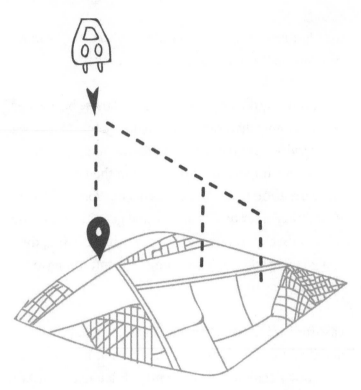

Why is this important?

When Google created Google Maps, the world was still thinking in terms of MapQuest and printing out directions on sheets of paper. People thought that a MapQuest digital map was an innovation, and it was. However, it was still a restricted, linear way to think about the implications of real-time location data. The world was still thinking in terms of creating a "better map." MapQuest didn't see the possibilities for the Ubers, the Airbnbs, the food delivery services, and the "on-demand" economy, which would totally reshape our lives. Google Maps did.

That's why we're here.

GET READY, BLOCKCHAIN IS ~~COMING~~ HERE!

Blockchain is the technical backbone of bitcoin and other cryptocurrencies. In the coming digital revolution, blockchain is going to change your life, even if you have no idea what it is. And that's the problem.

If you're like most people, you're confused about blockchain. It's a buzzword. You bought some bitcoin and made (or lost) some money. Your kid told you about it last Thanksgiving. Your boss mentioned that it's the next most important technology for digital transformation and insisted that you attend a few boring-as-hell conferences to learn about it.

But what does it all mean?

To answer that question and many more, this book will look at blockchain technology, its transformative potential, and its relation to bitcoin and other cryptocurrencies from many different perspectives. We'll look not only at the "Blockchain 101" nuts and bolts, but at its social and cultural causes and effects.

The way I see it, blockchain isn't just a technology. It's a technological manifestation of a social paradigm shift from centralized to decentralized, from siloed to open, from controlled to self-enforcing.

Blockchain is an emerging technology and, as with any other emerging technology, the market is confused about its relevance and applications. I'm inundated with invitations to speak to Fortune 100 company C-suites and boards of directors, and to provide keynote presentations at conferences for trade associations, governments, and large tech companies. I regularly educate corporate teams and share knowledge about blockchain on podcasts. The business marketplace is starving to know what's coming over the next digital horizon.

The market is confused about blockchain's relevance and applications. When evaluating it for their businesses, people often see it simply as a technology and ask, "Why is this important? Isn't it just a database?" They'll really start to see its value and understand its relevance only when they stop thinking in those terms.

Blockchain isn't just technology, much less a database, but represents a way of changing how business is done. It opens up silos and makes new ways of working with customers and other businesses possible.

I find a lot of interest in, but also suspicion of, blockchain. I'm asked, "Is this all just a load of bullsh*t?" Even informed technologists and executives doubt that block-chain will be a "seismic shift" in the ways we think about our finances, governments, food, relationships, and how we do business. They are unconvinced that blockchain will impact their industries. All too many of them don't see the need to think about it right now.

They're wrong. So. So. So. Wrong.

The reason I'm brought in to speak at conferences and businesses is not only to help industry leaders understand what the technology is, but also—and more importantly—how it is, in fact, relevant to them in their professional, business, and personal lives. I paint a picture that shows why they must start thinking about blockchain now, quite apart from the news stories about speculative cryptocur-rency investment and its impact on financial services.

BITCOIN AND BLOCKCHAIN

There's quite a bit of misinformation and misunderstand-ing about bitcoin and blockchain. There's a sense that blockchain is really only bitcoin, that the two are joined at the hip. It's true that blockchain was co-created with bitcoin, as the underlying technology for recording and substantiating bitcoin transactions. Some "bitcoin maxi-malists"—bitcoin true believers, if you will—are adamant that the two are, and will forever remain, joined at the hip. However, even if you look only at the many other cryptocurrencies and exchange-traded funds (ETFs) that have sprung up in the wake of bitcoin, it is clear that this is not true and was never really the case.

Disagree as the maximalists might, bitcoin is actually only the first use case for blockchain. It was the reason the technology was originally invented, but far from its only application.[2] The applications of blockchain—or, more broadly speaking, distributed ledger technology—go far beyond financial services into industries of all kinds. Blockchain is poised to affect almost every aspect of our personal and business lives. Since blockchain enables a set of protocols—like other well-known protocols such as TCP/IP and HTTP, which created the internet, the Visa network, and Google Maps—can you imagine what's coming next?

OPERATING SYSTEM OF THE FUTURE

This book's goal is to make blockchain technology relatable, to help you understand how it will impact you, your business, and your daily life. We'll also go into the broader sociocultural and political, as well as financial and economic, implications of its global adoption. We'll take a speculative, but informed look at the technology's

---

2   I use "invented" loosely here. Cryptography innovations such as Merkle trees were first proposed in the seventies.

revolutionary potential and how it is poised to change the world, not just in the next two to five years, but the next twenty.

They don't call this the fourth—or is it the fifth?—industrial revolution for nothing.

DISTRIBUTED LEDGER TECHNOLOGY

For most people, anything involving ledgers, however paradigm shifting, is likely to provoke a barely stifled yawn. But think again. Writing itself originated with account keeping! Seriously. In ancient Mesopotamia and other cultures, the first writing was a ledger tracking the seasons and planting of crops. Ledgers not only enabled the agrarian revolution, but also laid the groundwork for the advances in communications that made the industrial and digital revolutions possible.

What's important is not just the technology itself, but what it stands for: a global paradigm shift from data silos and monopolies to interoperability and interconnection. The appearance of blockchain is a unique moment in time, both in our ways of approaching data governance and as a key element in the convergence of new technologies such as big data, machine learning, AI, additive manufacturing, vertical farming, robotics, biotechnology, and the Internet of Things (IoT).

NETWORKS AND TRUST

The title of one talk I give is "Blockchain as the Operating System of the Future." When I say "operating system," am I talking about operating systems in computers? Am I talking about Linux or Unix? Not exactly. If we look beyond computing, we see operating systems in nature—representing anything from the nutrient cycle to ecosystems—and, more importantly, we see operating systems in our sociocultural, geopolitical lives. These socio-operating systems are exemplified by governments, culture, myth, tradition, social norms, and mores.

In other words, the operating system is a means of exchange, and in respect to blockchain, an operating system means both a social and technological compact. Blockchain, as an operating system, will not just change how we exchange money or do business, but will also impact how we make exchanges in the realms of finance, government, branding, and real estate, and generally how we relate to each other on a daily basis.

Blockchain is essentially a peer-to-peer technology capable of creating networks between individuals, databases, corporate entities, and countries: networks that can be trusted because, as you'll see, the technology eliminates the need for trust. Oxymoron alert! In other words, "Trust in trustless systems." But what does that mean? Blockchain is a technology that disintermediates middlemen (and women), eliminating the need for centralized clearinghouses, such as banks and governments, to verify transactions.

PROTOCOLS AND TRANSACTIONS

Another way of looking at blockchain is as a protocol or, more accurately, a technology capable of enforcing protocols. Let's back up. A protocol is essentially a means by which two or more parties interact with each other. Think of the word's use in diplomacy. When you get on the web to look something up on Wikipedia or send an email, you rarely if ever think about such underlying technical protocols at HTTP or TCP/IP, but they are what make the whole thing work.

Each blockchain creates a protocol or set of protocols that promotes a transaction, whether it's a financial transaction or a transaction of data, goods, or services. The blockchain protocol enables these peer-to-peer transactions because it can verify them. Transactions recorded on a blockchain can be trusted because they can't be altered or changed, and because the system is decentralized: blockchain records are replicated on every node in the network. However, blockchain protocols are not only technological, but create relationships and shared contexts, behaviors that shape and will continue to shape the social systems in which the technology functions.

WHAT'S THE WORD FOR IT?

We're still at such an early stage of emerging blockchain technology that we don't even have the language to describe what's going on. Blockchain is ultimately about creating a common consensus and shared knowledge. It's like defining a new color that you don't have the words for yet. It's all in the perception. A color can be conceived, but it also needs to emerge when other colors, shades, or tints are blended.

My background is in anthropology, semiotics, and linguistics, and, believe me, I just totally geek out on words. So, let's talk about "snow," a seemingly innocuous word. If you live in the northern latitudes, you're familiar with it, although in the south, not so much.

Anthropologists, cognitive scientists, and linguists have thought a lot over the years about what is called "linguistic relativity." I'll spare you the boring academic details, but the high-level premise is that language can—and does—shape our perception of reality. The "strong version" of the claim, which suggested that language structure determines how we perceive the world, has been mostly debunked by now. But let me relate an anecdote you may well have already heard.

A frequently cited, perhaps overused example of linguistic relativity comes from Franz Boas, one of the fathers of

American anthropology. Boas observed that the Inuit and Yupik languages, spoken near the Arctic circle, contain an unusually large number of words for snow. Hard snow. Wet snow. Slushy snow. You get the idea.

Now, if you've ever been skiing, you know that the English language, particularly at ski resorts, is also quite expansive on the subject of snow: Crud. Slush. Powder. Packed granular. Corn snow. Shred that gnar!

Not a skier? Perhaps you're a history buff, then?

A similar anecdote is told about the "invisible ships" phenomenon, which involves Captain Cook arriving in Australia by ship. Or was it Columbus in the Americas? As the story goes, the indigenous peoples, who had never seen a ship before, did not have a concept in their languages to construct that reality, and therefore didn't see the ships sitting in the bay.

Whether the tangible proof for these claims exists, or whether they're myths, the effects of linguistic relativity remain. In some schools of thought, words are said to shape reality. They certainly affect how we perceive and think about reality.

Words and myths are also shaping our new blockchain reality.

My background in anthropology and linguistics, as well as technology, flavors how I think about new words like "blockchain." As we've seen, blockchain originated in cryptocurrency and the exchange of cryptographic or encrypted assets such as bitcoin. A lot of the early language used to describe blockchain involved words like "wallet," "vault," and "tokens."

Is "wallet" the right word to describe a mechanism for storing and exchanging value? It's a common, simple word, which is good, but, ultimately, when I hear the word "wallet," I think of a brown, folding piece of leather that leaves an imprint in the back pocket of my dad's jeans. The word "wallet" may ultimately confuse as much as it defines and enlightens. It may make sense in the context of blockchain-enabled cryptocurrency, but may not make sense in other, non-financial contexts. The word "blockchain" might not even be the term that ultimately wins out, just as we use "internet" more often than the "web" today.

With blockchain and cryptocurrency, we're at a phase like that of the early days of the web: one of increasing awareness, education, and building a shared understanding. There's a lot of information already out there, but the real issue is knowing where to look for it and what is accurate or inaccurate. However, we already have a big advantage: the web has accustomed us to searching for and sharing information. You can go online and teach yourself about blockchain by reading a blog post, listening to a podcast, or getting your hands dirty trading cryptocurrencies.

MY BLOCKCHAIN OBSESSION

You can also read this book, written by a digital native, oh-so-millennial ex-hacker, and gamer, who studied social psychology at Oxford as a high school student, and anthropology and human-computer interaction (HCI) in graduate school, focusing her research on technology and society, particularly exchange mechanisms and virtual currencies in MMORPGs and virtual worlds. (That's "massively multiplayer online role-playing games" to you non-gamers.)

I'm also a serial entrepreneur who has started and run companies that leveraged the practical aspects of emerging technologies. I used to fly planes and skydive competitively, so I have a firsthand grasp of how physics works and how we might use physics to convert energy into money. (We'll get to that later!)

My first company was in apparel and textiles supply-chain and inventory-management systems. We built an AI-powered personal shopping system before buzzwords like "artificial intelligence" and "machine learning" came into common use. My third company, Chronicled, leverages blockchain to bring trust to global commerce and supply chains. My next company will remain a secret for now, but I assure you it's going to involve some of the concepts investigated in this book. The lack of true interoperability in our business systems has been increasingly frustrating, not just for me personally, but also for the enterprise in general, so I see blockchain's tremendous potential benefits in this respect.

Let's not kid ourselves, though. Technology is very powerful and has both positive and negative impacts. Social media has defined the second stage of the web, Web 2.0, whose positive effects were recognized almost immediately, but whose negative effects are only more recently coming to light. Tech-savvy, but increasingly skeptical thinkers like Jaron Lanier and Tim Wu shaped how I think about Web 2.0 and data privacy. I've always been a bit of a nut when it comes to data privacy, but it's surprising how long people traded convenience for, well, turning themselves into a product. In China, for instance, people's online behavior is directly linked to a social-credit score, which affects their ability to rent or buy a place to live, get a passport, and even purchase an airline ticket.

We need to be diligent, intentional, and conscientious in how we apply new technology and imagine the future. Both utopian "exponential transformation" and dystopian *Black Mirror*-episode visions abound, but in the day-to-day world, we need to focus on creating a realistic happy medium somewhere between the two. We need to have an open discourse in which we challenge each other and shape this future together. As with any powerful technology, once blockchain systems become entrenched, it will be difficult to change them. The time to start informing ourselves and thinking about this new technology is now.

The mission of my company Chronicled is to bring enterprise blockchain technology to supply chains, most notably via the MediLedger Project, a network for the pharmaceutical industry. *Newsweek* named Chronicled its Blockchain Impact Award winner for 2019, and *SF Weekly* named it San Francisco's Best Tech Company in 2018. My view is primarily from the enterprise-business-world trenches, but I believe we also need a larger perspective, which is where I've found an academic background, especially in anthropology, most helpful.

An observational, ethnographic perspective that involves embedding oneself in digital communities will be increasingly valuable as we move from the Web 2.0 of social communications to the Web 3.0 of digital transactions. This isn't an either/or, but a both/and scenario. Understanding background and history will help us envision new real-world models.

I feel so strongly about this that I decided to start speaking publicly about blockchain and cryptocurrencies and their convergence with other emerging technologies. I also blog on these subjects and write about them for *Forbes* magazine. I can't stop thinking about how this shift will not only impact the financial services industry and enterprise supply chains, but also transform the way we think about organizational models, work, distributed teams, and raising capital, as well as food production, additive manufacturing, education, entertainment, and the arts, with more to come. This book is the synthesis and current culmination of that process and my thoughts. We'll focus on both the practical side of things and imagining what this new technology can and will empower.

People often wonder how anyone can get as excited as I do about "distributed ledger technology." I get it. Accounting tools aren't sexy.

Well, screw those people. THIS TECH IS SEXY!

Recently—no joke—I was at a wedding between an actuary and a lawyer. It was so very dry until we hit the dance floor. Classic hits like Bon Jovi's "Livin' on a Prayer" and Kool & the Gang's "Celebrate" were staples. Then Whitney Houston's (RIP, Whitney) "I Wanna Dance with Somebody" came on. The actuaries—meaning all the groomsmen—went crazy! Break dancing, letting loose. Someone even said, "Actuaries gone wild!"

All this is to say, let's live a little. Accounting *can* be sexy. Accounting *can* be fun. Let's all be actuaries gone wild for a few seconds.

Which leads us back to ledgers. Ledgers *are* pretty badass when you remember that accounting was the basis of writing. Let your mind be blown.

This book will show you why "distributed ledger technology" will transform the way we live in the coming years and decades. The point is to help us all avoid short-sightedness and provide the knowledge, inspiration, and foresight to help us think creatively and differently about what blockchain and cryptocurrency are about to enable.

Let's get this Pizza party started!

PART I

BLOCKCHAIN AND BITCOIN: THE CHICKEN AND THE EGG

CHAPTER 1

A DAY IN THE LIFE JUST AROUND THE CORNER

The blockchain and cryptocurrency cryptography ecosystems—"ecosystem" is a word you're going to encounter a lot in connection with people who use this technology—are rich in memes. I could write a whole book on the crypto meme culture—expressions like "to the moon" or HODL ("hold on for dear life")—but we'll save that for another day.

ALICE AND BOB

One business-oriented meme involves two zealously overutilized stick-figure personas: "Alice and Bob." Alice is Ms. Average Jane and Bob is Mr. Average Joe. In cryptography, they are most commonly encountered as faceless humanoid icons or simple square boxes. I have no idea why the names Alice and Bob were chosen.

In all seriousness, the Alice and Bob meme touches on two questions. How are average people going to exchange value using cryptocurrency? Even more importantly, how is blockchain going to change their daily lives? Will they even think about it? Will they know that a seismic global paradigm shift and accompanying technological revolution are laying the groundwork for their lives? The underlying question is what our day-to-day lives are going to look like ten years from now, once blockchain and Web 3.0 have *transformed*—please, let's not say "disrupted"[1]—them.

Taking a historical perspective will again help us envision the new models that are emerging, so let's look at the recent past. We're already living in a world where web-based, two-sided marketplaces have become common.

---

1   "Disrupted" is a term that should never again be used in a pitch, sales deck, or general business vernacular. Ditto "digital transformation," "revolutionize," and so forth.

You only need to think of Amazon, which you probably use, either to get information or to make purchases, several times a day. What about travel? Ten or twenty years ago, you would have needed a travel agent to book a flight and find a place to stay while planning a vacation. Now, you have Travelocity, Kayak, and Airbnb, among many others.

THE DIGITAL LIFE

You can buy a plane ticket on your Delta app three hours prior to departure, check in via the app, add the ticket to your phone's wallet, grab an Uber, get to the airport, fly to a city you've never been to before, order a hotel room on a last-minute deals site, find the best restaurants on a recommendation site or blogs, buy a concert ticket for later that night on StubHub, take a photo with the performer, and upload it to your network of thousands of "friends."

Sound exhausting? It is. I can't personally attest to doing anything *this* spontaneous, but I can sure as hell tell you that it is comforting to have continuous access to on-demand booking when you show up in a foreign country, only to find your Airbnb booking was a fraud.

Like many millennials, I don't own a home, but live in an Airbnb I rent long term or short term, depending on where my work and speaking take me. Rather than buying a car, I use Zipcar or Uber to get from point A to point B. I have never had cable. Ever. I work where I want to work—in an office that is not an "office," but a shared or solo environment—where I have connectivity and balance. Personally, I'm not a fan of coworking.

More recent advances have already changed the landscape still further. With the Amazon app, you can have someone shop for and deliver your groceries from a nearby Whole Foods, while the Postmates app will order you lunch. If you need a doctor or specialist, you can find one on Zocdoc, a two-sided physician marketplace matching supply and demand.

There are new conveniences everywhere we look, and every time we use them, we pay the network or marketplace that is facilitating the interaction. However, when we move into a world that blockchain facilitates, the blockchain itself will perform the network's role, and we'll have become truly peer-to-peer.

Since Alice needs to get to work today, she calls Uber, and Uber contacts Bob, a nearby driver with a car. Uber is sitting in the middle of the equation. If a blockchain-based system were to take Uber out of the equation, the transaction would be solely between Bob as driver and Alice as passenger. Can Alice trust Bob and Bob trust Alice? In a non-blockchain world, hell no! Alice doesn't know sh*t about Bob. The dude could be a creep who wants to drive away with her in the car. Same goes for Bob: Alice could be a crazy, drunk passenger about to puke on his floor. However, in a blockchain world, given that all their previous transactions will have been unalterably recorded, this will no longer be an issue.[2]

STEPPING UP TO BLOCKCHAIN

Let's back up about an hour. Alice has just gotten up and goes into her usual workday-morning routine with soap, deodorant, and face cream. It's important to her that all the cosmetics and personal-care products she uses are paraben free. She currently "trusts" the labels on her products—which she knows is all greenwashing, but better than nothing—as well as the retailers who sell them. However, she soon will no longer need to trust the claims of the brands she uses or the retailers she buys from, since all of the products she buys will have blockchain-validated, paraben-free certifications.

(Are you a CPG—consumer packaged goods—brand or retailer? Scared yet? Want to put this book down and say f*ck that? Think again, my friends. If you can't beat 'em, join 'em, right?)

Why is this important? As convenient as two-sided, web-

---

2   I can't attest to blockchain solving the drunk-passenger problem.

enabled markets may be, they also open up opportunities for and problems with counterfeiting or diversion. The "fresh," "organic" shampoo you are currently buying from an online retailer may have been sitting on the shelf for a year or longer. The lettuce you buy from that premium-branded grocery store might have listeria or E. coli. Blockchain technology, on the other hand, can establish a "chain of custody" that guarantees none of this will be a problem.[3]

It's the same for the free-trade, non-GMO coffee Alice drinks after she gets out of the shower. Maybe she's out of coffee and runs down to the corner store to buy a twelve-ounce bag of beans. She can scan the bar code on the package with her smartphone and see the coffee's entire provenance: where it was harvested, where it was packaged and shipped, and whether it's actually "organic" according to a substantiated definition of the term.

Although Alice probably wouldn't do this scanning if she's part of an older demographic, let's imagine she is a millennial or even an oh-so-coveted Gen Z-er. Gen Z Alice will not only know how to use technology to retrieve synthesized and normalized data about a product, but will also know how to make sense of buying decisions based

---

3   I'm not a supporter of tracking lettuce on blockchain. I am, however, a huge proponent of blockchain-connected local transactional economies, CSAs (community-supported agriculture), and vertical farming.

on that data.[4] The other day I was getting a facial, and my esthetician told me about how Gen Z clients come in with full lists of enzymes and chemicals, and the products that contain them, that they are willing to use on their skin. This is an example of a peer-to-peer connection between producer and consumer.

A QUESTION OF TRUST

Let's think about the big picture.

Blockchain's paradigm shift will involve the disintermediation of "middlemen," whom we have, until now, relied on to play the role of "trusted" facilitator, connecting and verifying all the disparate parts of a network. Some examples:

- For our finances, we trust the bank.
- For our food, we trust the grocery store.
- For our information, we trust the publication.
- For our social connections, we trust the social network.
- For our education, we trust the school.

And the list goes on.

---

4   Gen Z Alice would also probably be named Arya, not Alice. The name of the badass character in HBO's *Game of Thrones* was the top female baby name in 2019.

We trust these parties because they provide the auspices of security, reliability, and comfort. We trust that they manage their vast, global supply chains safely, securely, and ethically. We trust their reputations.

To return to cosmetics, consumers will now begin their transactions farther upstream and closer to the source. They will no longer rely on the trust and ease retailers provide, the reputation brands provide, or the recommendations estheticians and other service providers make.

In the case most commonly cited in connection with cryptocurrency, consumers and institutions will move toward peer-to-peer transactions, trusting their currency to the blockchain as opposed to financial intermediaries such as banks. Alice will pay Bob for the ride to work through a direct transfer of value. Neither of them will any longer need to pay the premium that a bank-issued credit card imposes on one or both parties to a transaction.

In places like Dubai, Singapore, and even New York, drone delivery ports are increasingly being built into new buildings. How can Alice be assured that the computer she ordered is the one the drone delivers to her an hour later? Because all parties—human and machine alike—will be linked by a blockchain on which each link in the chain is unalterably validated.

Looking perhaps ten rather than five years into the future, as up-and-coming technologies, such as self-driving, autonomous vehicles become more common, the peer-to-peer relationship may well become one between passenger and vehicle. When Alice gets into the autonomous vehicle that's taking her to work, she won't have to worry that it's going to drive off a bridge. Then again, she might have to worry if her social-credit score is low and the car's AI makes a decision to save the life of a pedestrian with a higher score rather than Alice's.

Of course, there's much more to a transportation system than passengers and vehicles. There's what is called "the machine economy" or "machine-to-machine" interactions: vehicle-to-vehicle, vehicle-to-charging station, vehicle-to-parking garage, and vehicle-to-sensor. The autonomous vehicle that picks Alice up at her apartment will be electric, of course. Every time the car stops at a light, it will be sitting atop or near a radiant electric charging station that charges it for a minute or so, meaning it can keep going all day without stopping to plug in to a charger. Each electrical "fill-up" is a micro-transaction that the car itself pays for with a blockchain "wallet," which verifies the car's identity and makes the hundreds of such daily transactions that will need to occur feasible.

We can imagine a world where we send our idle vehicles out to work to earn "passive" income, a world where we no longer need to own vehicles, but can join an investment group that owns and operates a vehicle fleet.

We can imagine a world that goes far beyond the sharing economy, a world that creates entirely new concepts of personal property and ownership and enables never-before-possible business models and ecosystems.

SMART CITIES

At this point we've expanded beyond individuals such as Bob and Alice or you and me, and the commodities or resources we use on a daily basis, to larger smart-city networks and transportation grids. When I first got out of college, I lived on a particular block in New York and, in an attempt to save money, used air conditioning as little as possible, even in the middle of the summer.

My energy bill was still off the charts.

It turned out that, on my particular block, the electric company didn't meter electrical usage in each apartment or even each building. It measured usage of the entire block and then split the fees. It seems like most everyone else on the block kept their AC and lights on all day and all night. A blockchain-enabled energy grid, on the other hand, would both measure and manage my electrical usage on a granular level, down to and including individual appliances, which would then pay for their own energy, democratizing energy access and taking into account whether you're generating an energy surplus by using solar or a similar technology.

When it comes to blockchain-enabled smart cities, a favorite down-and-dirty example is trash collection. Since I live in New York City, I see a lot of trash when I walk down the street. Trash cans get put there, and the garbage just piles up until the one day a week the trash collection truck comes by. You could say that this is the protocol, social contract, or process that's currently in place. It's inefficient and ultimately unsustainable.

However, digitized "smart" trash cans could record usage and signal when they need emptying. Making that data interoperable between collection companies could enable a more efficient city-wide collection project, based on multiple companies' smart trash can IoT data. (The IoT, or Internet of Things, is based on inanimate objects such as trash cans collecting and tracking data.) Taking this a step further, a micropayment system would mean that if you don't have that much trash, you won't have to pay just as much as everyone else in your neighborhood to have it collected.

Decentralization is again key. There might be ten different smart trash can companies and ten different trash collection agencies. All the data generated by your and all of your neighbors' smart trash cans would be fed into a blockchain system that gives the agencies the ability to create the most efficient trash collection routes weekly, daily, and even hourly. Not all this data needs to be open, transparent, or fully shared. Competitors don't need to show all their cards. Blockchain technology will enable some of this data—only what is actually needed—to be accessed and leveraged by all of the collection agencies to improve everyone's efficiency.

ALICE AND BOB RETURN

Let's return to a typical day in Alice's current life. After work, she goes to the beauty parlor for a haircut and manicure. She wants to give her beautician a cash tip, but discovers she has no cash on her. She has to take extra time to run to the nearest ATM, which charges her a fee for the privilege of making a withdrawal from her bank account. A blockchain-enabled peer-to-peer app capable of disbursing small payments to service providers would disintermediate the bank and render her trip to the ATM obsolete.

The same scenario might occur when Alice stops by her local bodega, which only accepts cash, to get something quick for dinner. A blockchain-enabled, peer-to-peer app would cover the transaction, as it would any tipping in restaurants where Alice eats regularly.

Let's say that Bob wants to cook a fancy Saturday-night dinner for his wife, Alice. He's heard of the health and culinary benefits of wild-caught, fresh salmon and wants to get some for the dinner. Is the fish he buys really sustainably wild caught? Who effing knows? Blockchain to the rescue!

Say Alice and Bob decide to go to England or Thailand on vacation. Perhaps one of them needs to travel for work. As they travel, they will need to exchange one national "fiat" or government-issued currency, like the dollar, pound, or baht, for another. The value of each of these currencies fluctuates in relationship to one another.

The promise and potential of cryptocurrencies such as bitcoin is that their value will no longer shift in relation to the fiat currency of whatever country you find yourself in, providing a more stable, less volatile medium of exchange. Of course, Bob's cup of coffee might still be more expensive in Tokyo than it would be in St. Louis, but the goal of facilitating frictionless global payments will still be met.

PROTOCOLS AND SMART CONTRACTS

Protocols and "smart contracts" are two key concepts in both blockchain and cryptocurrency. Again, any peer-to-peer network depends on protocols, a shared behavior or social context codified in the network's technology. On the individual level, these protocols are implemented through smart contracts between or among all parties to a blockchain-enabled transaction.

The web runs on protocols such as HTTP and TCP/IP, which most of us never think about, but which are the foundation of the entire system. They permit me to receive, read, and respond to an email you send me. They permit me to write on my blog, log onto my favorite social network, stream my favorite movies and TV shows, play my favorite games, order my favorite foods (like Pizza, obviously), and access information on your website through my web browser.

More importantly, HTTP and TCP/IP allow my dad to send my brothers and me those dancing-elf video cards—you know, the ones with our cut-out faces on elf bodies dancing around to a song. They're like dancing actuaries gone wild merged with elves and crafty decoupage.

Early in the development of blockchain and cryptocurrency—in this case, "early" means 2016, and we sure as hell know that ain't early, but bear with me—Joel Monegro at Union Square Ventures proposed the concept of a "fat protocol," as a response to a critique of Ethereum, the second-most-prominent cryptocurrency system after bitcoin.[5] The argument was that the web we know and love was founded on "thin protocols" like HTTP—a single protocol that serves as the basis for a wide variety of applications. The system's value was generated and stored in these applications, particularly in the data generated, captured, and stored by such web giants as Google and Facebook.

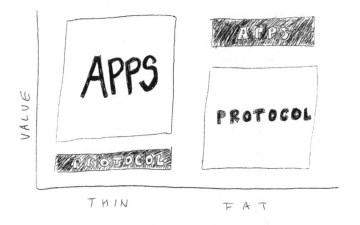

In contrast, it's possible for each and every blockchain to be built on its own "fat protocol." This means that, in this proposed scenario, there will be no, or only limited, interoperability among different blockchains. Each will be built on its own protocol meant for the exclusive use of the very few applications it enables. The blockchain's protocol, rather than its applications, generates and stores value.

---

5   Joel Monégro, "Fat Protocols," Union Square Ventures, August 8, 2016, https://www.usv.com/blog/fat-protocols.

Without going down the rabbit hole of debate about the pros and cons of the fat protocols thesis, the fact remains that, at this point in the technology's development, we're seeing the creation of many different protocols. Just like there were internet browser wars—remember, if you're old enough, AltaVista, or how the first version of Microsoft's Internet Explorer attacked and decimated the much-beloved Netscape Navigator?—we're probably going to be entering a period of protocol wars. There already exist, and are going to be hundreds more, companies involved in protocol development.

Some blockchains and their protocols may focus on the secure and frictionless exchange of cryptographic assets and cryptocurrencies, such as—ahem—bitcoin. Other protocols enable creative licensing and royalty management, solving the problem of how the musicians who wrote and recorded a popular song can receive micropayments that will properly compensate them for their work—something that is not yet possible and has created a crisis in the artistic community. Other protocols will track, validate, and establish a secure "chain of custody" for the flow of goods along supply chains. You get the gist.

"Smart contracts," as recently mentioned, are what govern individual transactions or groups of transactions within a blockchain. One way of looking at a smart contract is as the application of a blockchain protocol on a transaction-by-transaction basis. Many different smart contracts will enable and govern each step or "bit of functionality" in an overall transaction.

Returning to the salmon dinner Bob wants to prepare Saturday night: he uses a blockchain-enabled delivery app to buy the salmon, certified as wild caught, and then orders a drone to drop it off at his apartment. A sensor will record that the drone has entered his building and delivered the salmon, thereby triggering a payment from his account or "wallet." A smart contract governs each step along the way, defining the parameters that confirm that the delivery meets the "organic quality parameters" of the order and that the release and confirmation of payment have been properly made.

(This might sound crazy to you, but if you've ever met my stepmom, you'd know that she has her own "quality parameter protocol." When she opens a container of supposedly fresh spinach from Whole Foods that is even the slightest bit wilted, she'll return it. The above example is no different, aside from the automation involved, which will prevent such a transaction from occurring in the first place.)

Smart contracts and the blockchain protocols from which they are derived will achieve the end goal of automating decentralized, truly peer-to-peer transactions, along with social and business processes. It remains to be seen whether "fat protocols" will multiply with the creation of different blockchains, as Union Square Ventures advocated, or whether protocol standards will become established, with both winners and losers emerging from the "protocol wars." It's important to be able to speculate intelligently when dealing with powerful emerging technologies like blockchain, but impossible to read a crystal ball and predict what's going to happen with complete accuracy.

This brings us to a point that needs to be made several times, which is that transformative technologies may have both positive and negative effects. Alice has had a lovely morning washing her hair with paraben-free shampoo, drinking fair-trade coffee, and arriving safely at work in an autonomous, self-charging electric vehicle.

However, to take a dystopian *Black Mirror* perspective on what is happening, you could say that, since Alice might be drinking the same unbranded, blockchain-verified coffee as all the other people in her apartment building, she has lost some of the advantages of consumer choice.[6] Perhaps her genetic makeup has been analyzed, and she is given personalized supplements to take. These may make her healthier, but the entire pro-

---

6   Not that she had it in the first place. The corporations that once owned multiple brands created a similar illusion of choice.

cess has the potential of making her something of a cog in a blockchain-enabled wheel.

The serendipity and human interaction that are part of going down to the corner store to get something, discovering you have no cash, going to the nearest ATM, and returning to have a second interaction with the shopkeeper may be lost. Already at LaGuardia Airport, every restaurant has an iPad that enables you to both order and pay online, eliminating the possibility, for both parties, of a brief conversation with the waitstaff.

Blockchain is poised to make our lives better. But, as with some of the problems that have been emerging with Web 2.0, Bob and Alice, and you and I, need to be aware of and guard against the possible negative effects that may accompany any such advance.

{ CHAPTER 2 }

THE MYSTERIOUS SATOSHI NAKAMOTO

Back in 2013, the pseudonymous artist Banksy was in New York City for a thirty-day residency called *Better Out Than In*. Each night, the artist would produce a new work around the city and then give cryptic clues as to where the works were located. Many of the works were stolen within twenty-four hours of being unveiled. In 2018, Banksy sold a painting—an image of a girl reaching out for a heart-shaped balloon—for $1.4 million. Moments after the sale was complete, the painting self-destructed. Banksy, without revealing his, her, or their identity, has become massively successful.

There's power in mystery. And just like there are numerous conspiracy theories about who Banksy is, there are theories that Banksy IS Satoshi Nakamoto!

THE ORIGIN MYTH

Let's rewind.

Bitcoin and blockchain were created by a cryptic—pun intended—pseudonymous figure named Satoshi Nakamoto. Satoshi's real identity is still unknown, although there are many theories about who it might be. Was it an individual or a community?

Some informed guesses have identified the mastermind as leading cryptographer and computer scientist Nick Szabo, who created Bit Gold, often considered to be a direct precursor to the bitcoin architecture, in 1998. Others have identified Hal Finney, longtime "cypherpunk" and cryptographer, and the first bitcoin recipient, as the man behind the curtain. Finally, Dorian Satoshi Nakamoto, a Japanese American physicist and the only person in the US with the same given name, who lives in the same town as Hal Finney, is on the list of supposed members of the early bitcoin crew. Other individuals have made many claims on their own behalf, although none have been proven.

As they shouldn't. Because who the f*ck cares who created bitcoin? The thing *works*.

It's by design that no one knows who Satoshi Nakamoto is. She (or is it he or they?) is almost a religious figure. One popular T-shirt says "I am Satoshi Nakamoto." There's a meme image out there that mashes together the logos of Samsung, Toshiba, Nakamichi, and Motorola. Taken together, the first two to four letters of these companies spell out Satoshi Nakamoto. The words seem almost randomized, a set of characters put together to create a Japanese-sounding name, so the moniker could, in fact, be as ridiculous or obvious as an acronym or anagram of these big existing corporations.

The idea is that Satoshi is simultaneously everyone and no one. Most religions, nations, institutions, and associations have an origin story: look at the book of Genesis or the story of the Buddha's enlightenment. These origin stories aren't necessarily factually accurate, but exist more as archetypal narratives, myths, or images. Mentioning religious origin stories feels appropriate because cryptocurrencies link different groups or communities that have come together globally around a common set of beliefs.

In our commercially oriented society, brand origin stories about people joining together to found a company and produce or consume a certain product have become common. In the early days of Apple, and even today, people who used the company's products associated themselves with a creative mentality, in distinction to PC users and companies like Microsoft or Dell. PC users were a different demographic: business-oriented people who wanted to get a job done with as little expense as possible, rather than Apple's creative types.

How did bitcoin and blockchain start, and, even more importantly, when? In October 2008, "Satoshi Nakamoto" published a white paper on a cryptography mailing list—cryptography being a key element in the security and verifiability underlying all cryptocurrency and blockchain technology—titled "Bitcoin: A Peer-to-Peer Electronic Cash System." Does the date October 2008 ring a bell? The paper was published only a month after the greatest global financial meltdown since the Great Depression.

Coincidence? I think not. Satoshi wasn't just a brilliant technologist, but also a killer marketer.

RECOMBINANT INNOVATION

A strong case could be made for the assertion that bitcoin and blockchain were an example of recombinant innovation—innovation involving new combinations of previously existing elements—that came about in response to the 2008 financial crisis and the globalization leading up to it. Someone or some group came up with bitcoin as a way of meeting the impending financial meltdown.

Bitcoin was the first widely adopted implementation or "use case" of blockchain technology, which verifies and secures transactions independently of intermediary institutions like the big global banks. After all, it was the breakdown of these banks' high-stakes, increasingly abstract, and even unreal investment strategies that caused the entire international financial house of cards to tumble in the first place.

Blockchain also resulted from recombinant innovation. The Merkle tree, named after computer scientist Ralph Merkle, had been around since 1979. It is a set of interconnected or "hashed"—encrypted and thus secure—transactions, much like the chain of individual transactions or blocks linked together in a blockchain.

The basis for secure, distributed ledger technology had been around for a while. The concept of blockchain and the term "block chaining" go back to at least 1976, when authors William F. Ehrsam, Carl H. W. Meyer, John L. Smith, and Walter L. Tuchman published a paper called "Message Verification and Transmission Error Detection by Block Chaining."[1] They also invented cipher block chaining (CBC), where a record from the previous block is inserted into each subsequent block of plain text before being encrypted. Sound familiar?

Maybe we've had chains of blocks, as well as distributed ledger technology, for a while now. Why is everyone going cuckoo for crypto all of a sudden?

Ask any entrepreneur or business leader, and they will all tell you the same thing: technology is only one piece of the puzzle. Timing is everything. As the nineteenth-century French novelist Victor Hugo put it, "Nothing is as powerful as an idea whose time has come."

Cryptocurrency's time had come in 2008. People were feeling beaten down and were looking for alternatives to a financial system that had betrayed and, in many cases, pauperized them. One such alternative was bitcoin, which originated as a fist-shaking response to the collapse of business as usual.

---

1   William F. Ehrsam, Carl H. W. Meyer, John L. Smith, and Walter L. Tuchman, "Message Verification and Transmission Error Detection by Block Chaining," Google Patents, https://patents.google.com/patent/US4074066A/en.

Indeed, bitcoin early adopters—the initial bitcoin "ecosystem"—were a mix of crypto-anarchists, gamers, and hacktivists, as well as the occasional forward-thinking finance bro looking to make a quick buck on arbitrage schemes. Setting up a system at odds with the international norm was a very intentional move. The irony, of course, is that cryptocurrency soon evolved past and beyond the revolutionary impulse to a point where it was not necessarily at odds with the mainstream financial system, but actually began complementing and supporting it, becoming a parallel market, if you will.

However, in the beginning—to return to the origin story—the bitcoin community was composed of hacker cyberpunks and other folks who spent way too much time on Reddit. I remember when my brother used his *World of Warcraft* Alienware gaming-rig PC to mine bitcoin in the early days. That was some weird sh*t: the kind of stuff that, well, your parents yelled at you for, telling you to get off the computer and go play kickball with the neighbors. If only they had encouraged our basement mining operation instead.

However, bitcoin wasn't the first time technologically savvy outsiders became insiders and, in a few cases, the ultimate insiders. Look at Steve Jobs and Steve Wozniak, or Larry Page and Sergey Brin toiling away in their parents' garages.[2] The resulting pace of technological change had a transformative—call it disruptive if you must—effect on financial and other business transactions that the Harvard Business School crowd just couldn't keep up with.

BLOCKCHAIN AND THE INTERNET

It's also useful to look back at the earlier, related origin story of the internet and the web. The web wasn't a part of Ralph Merkle's original concept of the Merkle tree, as it didn't exist at the time. However, the truly distributed nature of blockchain technology wouldn't exist without it. One analogy, reported by Nick Paumgarten in his article "The Stuff Dreams Are Made Of," which appeared in the October 22, 2018, issue of *The New Yorker,* has compared the effects of blockchain to an imaginary clerk in nineteenth-century London making an entry in a ledger that would simultaneously appear in a ledger in Calcutta, the capital of British colonial India. That entry, once made, would be unalterable in either location. What would have been magic in the nineteenth century, the web has now made not only viable but commonplace.

Let's leave aside the fact that the internet was originally developed by DARPA, an arm of the US military, although there's much that might be said in this regard. Then again, I, perhaps like you, watch AMC's *Halt and Catch Fire* and

---

2   Ah yes, the mythical garage. I'm sorry, but here on the East Coast, we work in our basements!

still wish the internet had been developed in a garage by a group of rather incestuous friends.

When the internet became the web, with the advent of browsers, and started being adopted by the general public, there was a good deal of optimism about how the technology would give users completely unregulated access to a global information bank. That first glow of enthusiasm has long since been replaced with frustration and alarm that the data from our web interactions is being harvested by large tech corporations who are turning us—human users—into products, selling our data back to advertisers.

There's also the specter of governments and political organizations tapping into your data and violating your privacy. Edward Snowden, at this point still wanted in the United States and living in exile in Moscow, is an example of the type of hacker tech-head who felt betrayed by increasing centralization's violation of net neutrality and democratized, uncensored access to information. As we'll see in later chapters, one of the hopes of the crypto-anarchists who originated what is becoming the blockchain-enabled Web 3.0 is that this new technology will restore the promise of the early web through decentralization and assuring security and privacy.

Since Snowden himself is, to put it mildly, a controversial figure, as is WikiLeaks' Julian Assange, a larger point should be made here. There is an alternative blockchain and cryptocurrency origin story that asserts these technologies were originally created for use on the "dark web"—sometimes called the "Silk Road" and part of the "deep web" not indexed by search engines such as Google—as a means of facilitating illegal activities such as drug deals, clandestine payoffs, and even assassinations.

Frankly, that's total BS. Once you create the tech, others create the market. That's what happened with the dark web.

It's possible, even probable, that such "dark" transactions are taking place. However, the deeper impulse behind blockchain technology and the cryptocurrencies it enables is to fight the good fight of empowering individuals through truly disintermediated peer-to-peer networks. All of this is quite at odds with government surveillance and harvesting data for profit and influence.

The more complete blockchain origin story involves a response not just to the 2008 "Great Recession," important as that was, but to Web 2.0 and net-neutrality issues, as well as 9/11 and everything that followed: the Patriot Act, increasing surveillance, and the erosion of individual rights and privacy.

The mysterious anonymity of Satoshi Nakamoto is, in

my opinion, a very intentional positioning. The self-identified crypto-anarchists who originated, developed, and spread cryptocurrency and blockchain would not have been receptive to the idea of a leader or leadership group. This runs counter to the libertarian values they wanted to uphold.

And frankly, who gives a f*ck? I mean, why do we venerate "founders" as somehow messianic? It's time to move on and appreciate the movement beyond the person, however visionary, who may have kicked it off. Self-described visionaries are usually assholes anyways.

Yes, bitcoin has a fantastic origin story, in both senses of the word. It resonates emotionally and did what it was meant to do, which was to bring a group of early believers and early adopters together. In fact, the first bitcoin blockchain block was called the Genesis block.

People want to believe certain stories. That's human nature. We are a race of natural-born storytellers. The power of community is based on stories and myths like Washington and the cherry tree, which probably never happened, but has as much or even more influence on what Americans think they are as a nation than if it had happened.

Satoshi Nakamoto, whoever she, he, or they might be, is

the wizard behind the curtain who has created this magical world of Oz.[3]

To say that Nakamoto is really some computer scientist or the group of twenty hackers photographed having dinner together around the time bitcoin emerged is like telling people to stop believing in Santa Claus or the Easter Bunny. Pulling the curtain back would make the magic disappear. That magic lies in an origin story and its ability to bring groups of people together under the banner of decentralization and leaderless peer-to-peer networks.

At base, cryptocurrency and blockchain shouldn't need leaders to survive—or so we like to say. The computers on blockchain networks are doing exactly what they were designed to do: create consensus and provide trust or, more accurately, make trust unnecessary. The system was designed in such a way that it doesn't need—and shouldn't have—a leader, creator, or company that owns it and the data it generates.

Web 2.0 mega-applications like Facebook or Google can basically curate your entire life experience without you even knowing it. That's because they have the centralized authority that gives them access to your deepest data and the ability to make you see only certain news, buy only

---

3   L. Frank Baum's *The Wonderful Wizard of Oz* was originally written as a sociopolitical critique of currency (oz. or ounce) and East and West Coast banks. I suggest giving it a reread.

certain products, or vote for only certain candidates. Of course, you can learn about all this if you do the often-difficult research needed, but until recent investigations made everyone sit up and take notice, few people did.

Similar research into blockchain and cryptocurrency transactions is also possible, with one essential difference: anonymity. Yes, you can track down every blockchain-enabled transaction that has ever occurred, but you can't discover the identity of the individuals who made those transactions. You don't see the person; you just see a set of indecipherably randomized numbered characters. What you would find, both literally and figuratively, is a hash, which is a code almost impossible to decipher.

Of course, your identity might be tied to a wallet address, but you can have hundreds of wallets. The security that blockchain technology gives you is relative, but this relativity is extremely important. If you had the cryptography and technical skills, you could probably track back to the Genesis block of the bitcoin blockchain. However, this would be a very nontrivial problem, in contrast to how trivial it is to harvest the data you supply to Web 2.0 applications like Google without even thinking or realizing you are doing so. Tracking down the data in a blockchain block is hard, and that difficulty increases exponentially with every additional block you try to decrypt. There is a difference between what we can do if absolutely necessary and what we are really capable of or want to do.

WHO IS SATOSHI?

Before moving on, let's make one more attempt at identifying Satoshi Nakamoto, the woman, man, wizard, alien, or who knows what behind the curtain, the writer of the first bitcoin white paper and creator of the Genesis block of the bitcoin blockchain. Although some mysteries, like this one, are more powerful if left unsolved, the tendency to try to solve them is a natural one.

In 2015, there were two investigative pieces, in *Wired* and Gizmodo, that proposed that Australian computer scientist and businessman Craig Wright may have been the inventor of bitcoin. This case is particularly interesting, since Wright himself has claimed to have invented bitcoin, and this claim made him party to a $10 billion lawsuit the estate of his late brother, Dave, brought against him. His claim has been met with intense criticism from the cryptocurrency community.

As we'll see, there is a strong connection between online gaming and cryptocurrency, and online participants in role-playing games are strongly connected to the intended purpose of avatars, which is, above all, to hide one's "true" identity or to make it irrelevant. Unmasking oneself undermines and can even destroy the rules of the game.

Cryptographer Nick Szabo, another primary candidate— let's get real, *the* primary candidate—for being "the man behind the curtain," is a different case, one much more in keeping with some of the original impulses behind cryptocurrency. It's possible and even probable that, even if he isn't Satoshi, he was one of the brilliant cryptographers who got involved in the early development of blockchain technology. He coined the term "smart contract" and, as previously mentioned, developed a decentralized digital currency called "Bit Gold" in 1998. While that technology was never implemented, it served as a "direct precursor to bitcoin architecture."[4] Unlike Wright, he's made no claim to being Satoshi, but has spoken and written quite a bit about the technology. There have been several attempts to show, on textual grounds, that he wrote the original bitcoin white paper published in October 2008, but all of them have been inconclusive.

Several other candidates for the role have been put forward. However, the real identity of Satoshi Nakamoto, if there is such a thing, remains unknown. All we know is that his is a Japanese-sounding, and therefore inten-

---

4   Martin O'Leary, "The Mysterious Disappearance of Satoshi Nakamoto, Founder & Creator of Bitcoin," *HuffPost*, May 8, 2015, https://www.huffpost.com/entry/the-mysterious-disappeara_b_7217206.

tionally international, moniker. Satoshi is a first name given to Japanese boys that means "clear thinking, quick witted, wise." Nakamoto means "central origin" or "one who lives in the middle." For the time being, and perhaps for the foreseeable future, we'll have to leave it at that.

CHAPTER 3

BLOCKCHAIN: MUCH MORE THAN BITCOIN'S BACKBONE

I recently had an experience with the Wikipedia Mafia. Wikipedia is supposed to be a community-generated encyclopedia, right?

Wrong.

It's the centralized, crazy stepchild of Web 2.0's attempt to create a free and open information source. I might get harassed, blacklisted, or worse for writing this, but f*ck it.

What's my problem with Wikipedia? The platform appears to be open. Any public contributor can add content, but there are gatekeepers with reputations who have editorial and approval privileges and who run sketchy services that charge for posting content on the site. It's a mess and the perfect example of why the system is broken.

It wasn't always that way. Wikipedia was founded on many of the same ideals as bitcoin and blockchain: decentralization, libertarianism, and free-market capitalism. The idea was a platform providing community-curated information.

What happened, however, was that Wikipedia moved toward its centralized gatekeepers. Perhaps it was just too early for decentralization, or perhaps the system lacked proper governance. Whatever the case may be, Wikipedia was and continues to be a historical benchmark of supposed decentralization.

Blockchain is a relatively new technology that will probably transform the way we perform transactions of all kinds, including financial transactions. When people first hear about blockchain, which is the technical backbone of cryptocurrencies like bitcoin, but has tremendous potential in other fields, they ask the very natural question: what is a blockchain and how does it work?

If only there were a simple, easily understandable answer. I've sat in rooms at conferences and heard people give highly technical "Blockchain 101" talks that make the eyes of virtually everyone attending glaze over.

Part of the problem is that we haven't yet found the right explanatory metaphors or analogies. People in the industry say, "It's kind of like Wikipedia or a Google Doc," but there are several reasons that response is inadequate and even confusing.

First, the analogy gives a circular definition, explaining one type of software in terms of another. Yes, there is some similarity, because Wikipedia and Google Docs allow more than one person to access and add to a document. However, Wikipedia and Google Docs, all appearances to the contrary, are also essentially centralized systems, and probably the most important feature of blockchain is its decentralization and disintermediation of third-party middlemen, whether they be for-profit corporations like Google and banks, nonprofit institutions like the Wikipedia Foundation, or governments.

LEDGERS AND ACCOUNTING

Listeners sometimes perk up when I call blockchain "really badass accounting software" because people think that anything "badass" must be interesting. But this description doesn't really explain much in itself. Calling blockchain a "distributed ledger" is more accurate and conveys a lot more information, but the description isn't very sexy or compelling.

Recall, however, that writing itself was first developed to keep accounts, and then consider how writing changed the course of human history. Remember that even people who find ledgers and accounting completely boring are usually interested in how much money they have in their bank accounts.

Remember actuaries gone wild.

Ledgers are everywhere. I walk through a room in my apartment where the lights are on. If I thought about it for a moment, I'd recall they are being lit by electrical energy. If I had magic glasses on, I'd be able to see the ledger behind the lights. The electric company is recording how much energy is being used and what they are charging for it. With my magic glasses, I could look at every appliance in my kitchen the same way.[1]

There are also records, written or unwritten, of every article of clothing in my closet, every piece of furniture I use, everything I've bought and sold, and everything I own. Every time I go to the grocery store and look at the grocery list, that's a ledger. When I bump into a lady as I walk out of the store, and we both briefly size each other up to make sure neither party is angry, our system of checks, credits, debits, inputs, and outputs is also a ledger.

---

1   Or not-so-magic glasses. While Google Glass was a bit of a false start, with the rise of cloud computing and gaming, we'll see innocuous and even stylish augmented- and virtual-reality glasses soon entering the market.

A good friend who is an artist and ran her own gallery found that bookkeeping was the most interesting part of the job and decided to go into accounting. That's pretty unusual, but the fact is that there's accounting in every part of our lives. An artist in a gallery needs to keep track of not just the money that flows in and out but the paintings hanging on the walls or sitting in the backroom, as well as any other registered assets. "Accounting" and "ledgers" are just the way our brains work.

What makes a blockchain a special, innovative ledger is that it is distributed and cannot be changed. I suppose I could put my shopping list into a blockchain, but there would be no reason to do so. Nobody else needs to know what I'm going to get at the market (except in the unlikely case that being at the market at a certain time might supply an alibi that I wasn't somewhere else committing a murder or other crime).

When a transaction is entered into a blockchain ledger, after being checked for accuracy, it is automatically written on every copy of the ledger—the blockchain—that exists everywhere in the world, whether it be New York, Peoria, Seoul, or Nairobi. Once it is written, it cannot be altered. It becomes what's called an "immutable record." What makes this possible, of course, is the web, and what blockchain is going to make possible is a transformation of the Web 2.0 of social media to the Web 3.0 of secure, disintermediated transactions.

A blockchain stores the data involved in every transaction or "block" of which it is made. However, while blockchains are often compared to databases, which are essentially structured, digital, data-storage containers, the differences between a blockchain and a database are as important as the similarities. A blockchain is a network that shares or distributes data or proof of data. Just as importantly, the data stored in a blockchain must be validated and made impossible to tamper with before it can be, or is, shared. It is an immutable ledger or list of transactions, something that is not true of normal databases.

How do you know that the data being stored in a database is accurate? You have to have a reason to trust the database, which generally comes back to trust in the institution that has created it. You may not entirely trust the banking system, but you trust the bank where you keep your checking account enough to deposit your paychecks there. You may have reservations about the government and probably don't like paying taxes, but you trust the Federal Reserve banking system enough to accept a twenty-dollar bill from someone you have just sold something to. They also trust it enough to accept the $1.40 in change you give them back, along with the item they just purchased.

CODE AND CRYPTOGRAPHY

Here's where things get technical. (I promise, it won't be too painful.) Many people think that, in order to understand blockchain and cryptocurrency, they have to understand the technology behind it. Then when they encounter a "Blockchain 101" talk or book, their eyes glaze over.

As I've said many times, it's much more critical to understand the social and business shifts blockchain is making possible. Still, there's no denying this is a relatively new and complex technology. It's good to have some technical background, but not to get hung up in it, especially if you don't have a computer science background. Hang tight while I do my best to present you with a happy medium between "just the basics" and going down a black hole of techno-speak.

Blockchain technology's greatest innovation is disintermediated distribution: eliminating the need to trust a third-party guarantor of the validity of a transaction. How is this possible? There are several mechanisms for making this happen, all involving some form of cryptography. The data in a blockchain transaction is coded with a form of cryptography known as "hashing." We'll spare you the details here, but if you're interested, there's plenty of information about the process on the web or in computer science courses.

The proof that a transaction is valid involves the ability to decode or "solve" the code in such a way that its accuracy is assured. The transaction's immutability—the fact that it can't be changed—is built into the code as an essential element. If the transaction code is altered or inaccurate, it can't be properly decrypted, so the transaction is rejected and not made part of the blockchain network.

Each time a blockchain is updated with a new transaction block, that transaction must be validated, verified, and time-stamped before being distributed throughout the network. Given that there is no third-party validation of the transaction, it's critical to make attempts at falsification impossible or nearly so: this is part of the core architecture of any blockchain network.

PROOF OF WORK AND PROOF OF STAKE

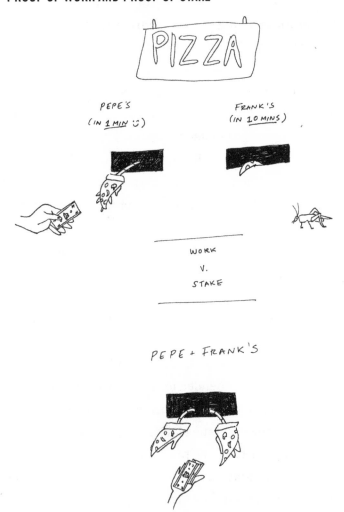

As with most cryptography and software engineering, which is called coding for a good reason, this is where things get very technical and complicated. Rather than going down a rabbit hole that will only lead, for most of us, to more confusion, let's just say that two of the main algorithms for verifying blockchain transactions are known as "proof of work" and "proof of stake."

Proof of work was and is the means of validation employed by bitcoin, the first cryptocurrency and, according to its devotees—bitcoin's "maximalists" or "fundamentalists"—still the only valid use of blockchain technology. The fact remains that there are many other blockchains that are ledgers or records of other types of transactions, whether of non-bitcoin cryptocurrencies, real-world assets, or even registers able to verify an individual's identity.

Proof-of-work validation is performed by so-called miners or block miners, essentially computers that decrypt or solve encrypted or "hashed" information in a transaction block intended to be added to the blockchain. To be validated, a block's hash must also contain the hash encrypt of the previous block in the chain, as well as a timestamp verifying the time of the current transaction. To ensure validation, the decryption must take place within a strict ten-minute time limit.

All these requirements—those described here, while fundamental, just scratch the surface—have been set up to guard against inserting invalid blocks into the blockchain, such as counterfeit copies of previous transactions meant to subvert the system. The integrity of the blockchain could be compromised, for instance, by allowing someone to spend the same bitcoin twice. This is such an important issue that it has its own name: "the double-spending problem."

Proof of work, although it does the job of validating transaction blocks extremely well, requires a good deal of computing power, and therefore uses a lot of energy, a major problem and drawback. Miners tend to be located in places where energy is relatively inexpensive, such as Iceland or China. In fact, a huge Chinese company called Bitmain, which at its peak posted annual profits of $4 billion, manufactures computers specifically for mining purposes, runs the world's largest mining pool, and seems poised perilously close to becoming a monopoly.

Other forms of validation, such as "proof of stake," have therefore been developed or proposed by alternative cryptocurrency systems such as Ethereum. Proof of stake involves a variety of mechanisms by which the designated originator of the current block in a blockchain already participates or has a "stake" in the blockchain and is therefore very unlikely to undermine their own self-interest through falsification. Temptations to attack the validity of a blockchain by falsifying a block still exist, and a number of variations of proof of stake have been and are being developed to overcome the methodology's potential security problems. Most of the large-scale cryptocurrency operations, even including Ethereum, still operate on proof of work.

KEYS AND ORACLES

While blockchains are created to provide security and verifiability, nothing is absolutely infallible. When you make a bitcoin transaction, it goes from your wallet, which is encoded with a unique private key, to someone else's wallet, encoded with its own private key. Since you don't and can't know the other wallet's private key, the transaction has to pass through a public key, an unhashed version of its private key. If I enter someone's public key, or someone enters mine, incorrectly, the transaction wouldn't take place as intended. It might end up somewhere entirely different, and, given the inalterability built into blockchains, it is unlikely that the mistaken transaction could ever be undone.

Currently, many exchanges manage users' keys with a centralized, custodial key-management solution. People choose to do this for any number of reasons, most having to do with the challenges of securely storing keys.

Other potential problems enter when the transaction involves something in the "real world," such as a business or personal asset, rather than a cryptocurrency. What is called an "oracle" needs to be brought into the process to verify any necessary data or information generated from outside the blockchain system. This could be something as simple as a database containing information about the current temperature, say, or the amount of wear on a car's brakes, or even the car's make, model, and year.

As this information comes from outside the blockchain network, it's possible that this data could be manipulated or falsified and therefore poke a hole in the blockchain. Such oracles, with their potential to be manipulated or falsified, are going to become increasingly common with the advent of the machine economy and Internet of Things: the increasing use of robotics, autonomous vehicles, additive manufacturing, wearable technology, and monitoring chips within physical devices such as appliances.

These are the sorts of arguments that bitcoin and other cryptocurrency fundamentalists bring up when asserting that there is no such thing as non-bitcoin or non-cryptocurrency blockchain. However, the cat's already out of the bag: the potential and ability of blockchain technology to disintermediate third-party verification will continue to be applied to more and more non-bitcoin and non-cryptocurrency transactions. Infallibility is a goal that will never be reached: the challenge is to bring security and verifiability to within tolerable limits.

ENTERPRISE BLOCKCHAINS: PRIVATE AND PERMISSIONED

So-called enterprise blockchains are stepchildren of the original public cryptocurrency blockchains. Pragmatic businesspeople are generally interested in the application of this technology to their enterprises because its functionality improves on current systems. It adds value, given the current fragmentation of enterprise systems, data, and software, and blockchains' potential for facilitating new methods and types of inter-company commerce. No one is claiming or even aiming for absolute infallibility in enterprise blockchains, which are already working fairly nicely.

There is no question that crypto fundamentalists will take issue with this. Quite a few will go so far as to say permissioned blockchains are bullsh*t. In some ways, I sympathize with and even tend to agree with them. Of course, having a blockchain network governed by a single, large, blue-chip IT company doesn't solve many problems. However, creating and using blockchains outside cryptocurrency exchanges is a fact of life that's here to stay, and, as mechanisms to manage, govern, and expand permissioned networks evolve, we will see an explosion of enterprise networks set up to facilitate industry resource planning (IRP).

True believers and radicals thrive and are probably necessary in environments where powerful new technologies are created. Today's battle between Apple's macOS and Microsoft's Windows is nothing like it was in the late eighties, when the controversies over the pros and cons of the two operating systems and over vertical integration versus open systems were at the boiling point. As developing technologies become more developed, compromise is inevitable.

Cryptocurrency blockchains are "public blockchains." This means, for example, that the bitcoin blockchain is open to anyone who wants to buy a bitcoin.

There are two alternatives to public blockchains: private blockchains and what I like to call permissioned blockchains. A private blockchain is under the control of a single business or entity, which manages and controls access to the blockchain. I feel cryptocurrency fundamentalists have a point when they say that such blockchains, although they incorporate important aspects of the technology, aren't really blockchains at all. They are, instead, fundamentally old-fashioned database networks built on a new consensus mechanism.

IBM, for instance, has created a number of blockchains, including one called the Food Trust blockchain. Although they are being marketed as blockchains, they are still completely centralized, which just doesn't compute. IBM, which is not the only major corporation creating private blockchains, or what's called Blockchain as a Service (BaaS), has control over every node or block. These are not peer-to-peer distributed networks, but something more like IBM Cloud services solutions. There is certainly a place for IBM Cloud services, but let's call a spade a spade. A genuine blockchain's node operators are distributed, not centralized.

On the other hand, a permissioned blockchain is one that permits a certain set of white-listed individuals to join and participate in a network on a conditional, such as "read-only," basis. Further permissions are required to write data on the network. White-listed parties can access and read certain data on a permissioned blockchain, but only a few of these parties have permission to add blocks. Again, unlike Wikipedia or Google Docs, once a block has been added to the chain—once data has been written on the network—it's immutable and can't be changed.

This model has value in a lot of different use cases. It works well, for example, in a regulatory environment. My company Chronicled built a permissioned blockchain network called MediLedger so that pharmaceutical companies, who compete with one another in most respects, can support each other in the one important instance of maintaining regulatory compliance. More on this later.

Permissioned networks work well whenever audit trails

are needed. They help industries in which companies work with other companies they don't necessarily trust, since they can create a layer of shared trust and verification missing from current databases.

Many of the transactions sketched in the previous chapter, "A Day in the Life Just around the Corner" will be made possible by permissioned networks. They can create the multiparty protocols and smart contracts that multiparty networks of all kinds will need in order to function. Permissioned networks will automate, support, and enforce contracts and regulations across different organizations, particularly among enterprises and between enterprises and their customers.

WEB 3.0 VALUES

Despite my previous involvement with permissioned blockchains, I'm sympathetic to public-blockchain maximalists in many ways. The idea of being able to make a transaction that can be verified, but not be tracked by third parties is powerful. A protocol called Orchid has been proposed to rebuild the internet itself with blockchain-type mechanisms that will enforce privacy and net neutrality. These are values and features that internet pioneers like Tim Wu and Jaron Lanier are very passionate about and feel have become increasingly important the more they have been superseded and violated in the social-media-based Web 2.0. Maybe blockchain-based Web 3.0 will lead to a new beginning for the internet.

There's a reason for the tribalism of bitcoin maximalists. They advance many of the same arguments that were made in the early days of the web. Is the internet, or should it be, a censorship-resistant universal data-sharing tool? Is it a digital library or something much more? Web 1.0 evolved into Web 2.0 in large part to realize the internet's commercial aspects, its ability to facilitate commerce, then advertising, and then—call this evolution or devolution—to capture people's attention and time.

Cryptocurrency arose in opposition to this fairly natural, but not always desirable evolution. As we've seen, it was implemented in large part in opposition not only to the existing financial system, which led to the global instability of 2008, but also to what the internet itself had become. It's hardly unexpected for controversies to arise as powerful new technologies with tremendous untapped potential emerge. It worries me to see big blue-chip corporations claiming to own or be able to sell you a blockchain. That's fundamentally opposed to what a blockchain—and the sociocultural paradigm shift it represents—really is.

Fundamentalists may have some very valid points, but the world isn't a simple place. However, to understand both cryptocurrency and blockchain, which began as bitcoin's technical backbone, you have to understand why we want or need decentralization: a truly peer-to-peer ecosystem—such as a nation-state, enterprise, bank, healthcare system, and so forth—where our interactions, communications, and financial or other transactions are not facilitated through a third party.

At the same time, this complicated technology is easily misunderstood and therefore misused. There are advantages to having regulators involved, giving people advice on what should and should not be done. No one wants to get arrested for getting involved in a misunderstood frontier technology.

However, bitcoin and other maximalists would violently disagree with this perspective: "You shouldn't even care about regulators. Keep them out. The bitcoin blockchain was created so that government and regulatory agencies can't track your transactions." This is how cryptocurrencies got the reputation of being the dens of drug dealers, gamblers, assassins, and other criminals.

But blockchain is so much more than that. I believe that privacy is a fundamental human right and should be respected in all aspects of our lives, from our internet browsing habits to our financial transactions, medical data, and DNA information.

Let's look at an example that demonstrates the problem with centralized parties controlling access to valuable personal identification data.

During Hitler's reign, IBM's Hollerith machine provided census data, punch card data, and other data to the National Socialist Party (Nazis). While neither IBM nor the technology itself were at fault, the technology was in part responsible for the systemic extermination of millions of people.[2]

Now think for a second. Whom have you given personal identification information to?

Perhaps you've provided your genetic makeup and DNA data to an ancestry service that has collected your DNA. Well, that company is probably selling that data to your insurance company, which is, in turn, raising premiums based on genetic likelihood for heart disease.

Have you bought a smart toothbrush? (Seriously, they exist.) It's tracking how often you brush your teeth and also selling your data to the same insurance company. What about the Fitbit or Apple Watch you wear? Are you starting to get the idea?

Perhaps you use email, a browser, a search engine, or an

---

2   Edwin Black, *IBM and the Holocaust* (Washington, DC: Dialog Press, 2012).

operating system. In fact, you almost certainly do. Those companies are tracking everything from your emails, to your browsing history, to your odd obsession with Taylor Swift.

As part of the distribution of its 2019 anthology series *Love, Death & Robots*, Netflix supposedly utilized an algorithm that ordered the episodes based on the viewers' sexual orientation. While Netflix has refuted the claim, the concept of targeting content, products, and other advertising products based on demographic information is nothing new.[3]

Data collected based on your shopping habits at the local drugstore or grocery store informs algorithms, which, in turn, inform which "coupons" are printed out at the cash register. Upon your return to the store, those "coupons" will direct you to a certain aisle to pick up that product, often leading you through a maze that brings you past your most commonly purchased products. And this is just in-store. Think about the data collection and advertising game going on online.

My point is: think twice about what you are giving away on a daily basis and to whom. If you don't want to do all

---

3 Natalia Winkelman, "Netflix Clarifies Love, Death & Robots Episode Sequencing: 'This Is a Test'," *Slate*, March 19, 2019, https://slate.com/culture/2019/03/netflix-love-death-robots-episode-order.html.

the work involved in thinking twice, remember what can happen—in the most extreme cases—when centralized authorities control all your data.

Okay, enough with the heavy sh*t. It's a lot, I know. Let's get back to what we can do to rectify this.

BACK TO THE FUTURE

On the far more positive side, I genuinely believe block-chain is the operating system of the future. I wouldn't be spending all this time writing a book and not eating Pizza and drinking Cab if I didn't believe in it. Let's look back in time to understand where we were, how we got here, and where we're going. Join me in traveling to the earliest version of the network: the village.

If I lived in a village my whole life, and my shoes needed mending, I'd take them to the local cobbler, someone I saw almost every day and knew I could trust. If I was an apple farmer and it was still early summer, I could say, "If you fix my shoes, I'll give you a bushel of apples as soon as they're harvested." The cobbler would almost certainly agree to the deal, and we'd record this on some sort of written or verbal ledger or with a handshake.

Sounds good in theory, right?

Well, what if the cobbler wanted to buy leather? If he accepted my apples and then had to try to exchange those apples for leather, things could become incredibly complex. What if the tanner didn't want apples, but eggs? In *Debt: The First 5,000 Years*, which explores the historical relationship of debt and social institutions, David Graeber states:

> The definitive anthropological work on barter, by Caroline Humphrey, of Cambridge, could not be more definitive in its conclusions: "No example of a barter economy, pure and simple, has ever been described, let alone the emergence from it of money; all available ethnography suggests that there never has been such a thing."[4]

Apparently, there never was a barter economy. It's yet another myth, like the mystery of Columbus's boats. I never gave a cobbler apples for my shoes, but perhaps I did exchange a metal coin, token, chit, shell, dried trout, or tea block, depending on my location.

Perhaps I didn't exchange anything physical at all, and the transaction was recorded on a written ledger as a series of credits and debits. According to Graeber:

> In this sense, the value of a unit of currency is not the measure of the value of an object, but the measure of one's

---

4   David Graeber, *Debt: The First 5000 Years* (New York: Penguin Books, 2014), 29.

trust in other human beings. This sort of debt-token system might work within a small village where everyone knew one another, or even among a more dispersed community like sixteenth-century Italian or twentieth-century Chinese merchants, where everyone at least had ways of keeping track of everybody else.[5]

Whether we were bartering in a fantasy barter-land, buying beers on credit at the local medieval pub, or selling fish in Newfoundland, we still relied on the trust of our local communities. We relied on the fact that we knew our creditor to some extent.

We have transitioned into a vast and complex global village, largely through the connectivity provided by the advent of the internet and other telecommunications systems, mobile phones, new manufacturing practices, and air travel. We now live in an exceedingly complex global network of information and supply chains. We've lost that level of trust in the individual as we've moved into a "global village" and placed it in the hands of social, financial, political, and other institutions.

Cryptocurrency and blockchain were proposed as a means of facilitating decentralized trust on a global scale. I call this system "trustless" because I no longer need to trust a cobbler two thousand miles across the world,

---

5   Ibid., 46.

or the reputation, brand, and logistics capabilities of the multinational retail conglomerate. I just need to trust the network to function properly by completing a valid transaction. To me, the blockchain is a global operating system not just in technological terms, but in terms of a global social compact. As you'll see in later chapters, blockchains will permit us to localize even as we continue to globalize.

Cryptocurrency and blockchain are systems that can facilitate global commerce in an entirely new way, neither mediated nor facilitated by the vast global supply chains, conglomerates, and large banks that contributed to the destruction of the global economy in 2008. Blockchains are poised to become globally accessible peer-to-peer networks that anyone can participate in, in order to communicate and make financial or other types of transactions, activities that have so far depended on centralized third-party mediation.

Above all, it's important not to think of this or any powerful technology as existing in a vacuum. Think instead in terms of convergence. Blockchain will intersect with current and other emerging technologies: empowering the Internet of Things (IoT) and the next level of machine learning and AI, as well as robotics, genomics, augmented and virtual reality, and additive manufacturing, among many others.

As the operating system of the future, blockchain really is the underlying protocol through which all these different systems will interact. It's especially important to think about all this now: how we're designing, architecting, and utilizing blockchain technology. The beginning, the low point in the stack, is where we really have the power to change things for the better—or the worse.

CHAPTER 4

BLOCKCHAIN: DECENTRALIZATION, GOVERNANCE, AND COMMUNITY BUILDING

How many of you have kids? Some of you must.

Let's work through a little thought experiment, envisioning something we'll call the Decentralized Autonomous Classroom. Instead of teachers, we have a room full of self-selecting kindergartners managing everything that happens. You'll very quickly see the kids congregate near their favorite classroom stations. The group that likes finger painting does finger painting. Some girls and boys are playing house. Some build with blocks, in a sandbox, or digitally on a laptop or iPad.

One kid suddenly throws a block at another's head. The tension rises and civil unrest builds, until one girl yells, "Boys are stupid!" The revolution has begun. She insinuates herself as the de facto leader of the supposedly decentralized autonomous classroom, and the kindergarten devolves into a millennial version of *Lord of the Flies*.

Now, let's explore how this thought experiment might apply in the real, adult world.

UTOPIA, DYSTOPIA, OR SOMEWHERE IN THE MIDDLE?

Each blockchain is a decentralized peer-to-peer network. With no centralized authority permitted, individuals—

the "peers" in the network—now manage their own data, assets, and identities, as well as build self-defined business, social, civic, and economic communities. Each community member has a "self-sovereign" identity. Network management is called "governance." The first blockchain use cases were global ecosystems focused exclusively on cryptocurrency financial transactions, but blockchain applications can and have expanded far beyond this initial focus.

Blockchain can be thought of both as a distributed ledger and a peer-to-peer system that allows community members to communicate and transact among themselves, without intermediaries or a central authority's oversight, permission, or interference. In a Decentralized Autonomous Classroom, the now-disintermediated central authority would be the absent teacher.

People naturally organize into communities based on selected affinities, forming what anthropologists call "communities of practice." We see this in the block throwers and finger painters of the Decentralized Autonomous Classroom, and even in a centralized marketplace like eBay. Soon after eBay's creation, niche communities arose among people who specifically wanted to trade handbags, baseball cards, classic automobiles, eight-tracks, vinyl records, Atari games, Magic the Gathering cards, and so on. After eBay provided the platform or marketplace and tools that enabled these transactions, these communities of practice sprang up almost immediately.

Of course, eBay isn't a true peer-to-peer system, but a centralized one that plays the role of trusted intermediary. This makes the user or customer experience frictionless and also enables eBay to charge fees for and harvest data from all network users and transactions. You place trust in eBay, confident you will receive the end product, that it will be high quality, and that your payment will be released. In exchange, whether you are a buyer or seller on the network, you give up some liberty and control. eBay oversees what you, as an end user, can and cannot access.

The point is that niche communities of practice are the natural result of any platform of exchange, whether intermediated or disintermediated. Community building is human nature, whether the underlying system is centralized or peer-to-peer. While creating communities of practice was probably not eBay's original mission, they inevitably sprang up after the platform was launched.

In contrast, any blockchain's mission consciously includes enabling such communities. The original bitcoin community was composed in large part of computer-literate cryptographers and scientists, hacktivists, libertarians, online gamers, high-frequency traders, hobbyists, and other affinity groups. They then went on to create other, similar communities of practice by building the next evolution of internet gaming, trading, and other platforms.

When it comes to human nature, however, nothing is simple or cut-and-dried. It's quite possible, for instance, that one of the early blockchain-enabled bitcoin communities was composed of criminals making illegal transactions outside the purview of "centralized" governmental or regulatory oversight.

But, alas, why must we keep dwelling on this? Criminals exploit our existing institutions in any number of ways. They launder money in plain sight through the world's biggest banks. They fuel illicit-trade markets, including forced labor on fishing vessels in international waters, where boats can't be apprehended. They burn rain forests to grow palms for palm oil. They exploit child labor in mica mines. They ship counterfeit goods across borders. They utilize alternative asset classes like fine art to exchange value across borders while avoiding tariffs.

Crime is a problem throughout our current system. Criminals bank at our biggest banks. Let's at least agree that criminal exploitation is widespread and stop using cryptocurrency as a scapegoat for criminal activity.

Decentralization restores the "self-sovereign" identities

many of us feel we have lost or are losing, because banks control who can and cannot make transactions, retailers control what we can and cannot consume, and browsers and search engines control what information we can and cannot access. The right to associate and enter into contracts with whomever we please is a central tenet of a liberal society, one that blockchain is able to support and bolster.

Blockchain is also interoperable with any number of other powerful emerging technologies, such as artificial intelligence, machine learning, quantum computing, and the Internet of Things (IoT). We are just beginning to construct an even more powerful infrastructure for transactions and communications. Its development is bound to take a lot of twists and turns along the way.

As with any emerging technology, there are both utopian and dystopian sides to blockchain. The unknowns outnumber the knowns.

We began this chapter with a hypothetical thought experiment: what would a Decentralized Autonomous Classroom look like? Educational reformers, believing children learn best when allowed to follow their own interests in relative freedom, have been advocating this concept for centuries, and, on the face of it, their philosophy makes a lot of sense.

Such utopian decentralization, however, might inadvertently lead to *Lord of the Flies* chaos. Giving kids the opportunity for creative expression could very well escalate from drawing on paper to marking up classroom furniture and walls, and then to a full-blown dystopia, with kids asserting authority over, exploiting, or harming their classmates.

THE STRANGE CASE OF "THE" DAO

Utopian and dystopian potentialities in blockchain are not necessarily either/or, but could be both/and, especially as the technology goes through its inevitable growing pains. This has already occurred with respect to the ideal of decentralization. The term "decentralized autonomous organization" (DAO for short), like the term "peer-to-peer," has a nice ring to it, and is in many ways a genuine ideal.

A DAO's rules are encoded in a computer program and are transparent to and controlled by shareholders rather than a government or other authority. Instead of a typically centralized organizational and management structure, where a board of directors makes key decisions then implemented by C-suite executives and on down the chain of command, a DAO structure is meant to act more like open-source code. A DAO charter allows any member to vote, in supposedly decentralized fashion, on key decisions, such as how much funding should be allocated to which projects.

The reality on the ground is more complicated, however. An early and particularly well-known example of a DAO was The DAO—yes, the terminology can be confusing—instantiated on Ethereum, the cryptocurrency platform created next in line after bitcoin. The Ethereum DAO was established to raise money through crowdfunding. The funds raised were managed by algorithms underlying the Ethereum virtual network or blockchain, rather than by individuals.

When The DAO was first launched, I wrote a white paper to determine whether it would be wise to invest in the project. I was mainly curious about analyzing and following the process, however, and my interest was repaid with interest.

The DAO was launched in May 2016, and a devolution into a *Lord of the Flies* scenario happened very quickly. A month later, members of The DAO "community" were able to hack a vulnerability in the code that siphoned off a third of the funds raised, about $50 million.

So much for decentralization. Or was it?

Communities, such as nations, have differences of opinion that can turn into squabbles and escalate into wars. Bitcoin maximalists continue to believe that bitcoin is the only legitimate blockchain use case. In some respects, they may have a point. Bitcoin was created by an anonymous individual or group and remains fundamentally leaderless. It was built to transcend government or state centralization, and because there is no leader—it is fully decentralized—there is no one whom government authorities could prosecute if they wanted to.

That said, bitcoin is, in fact, now largely controlled by its validators: bitcoin miners. As large mining operations control ever more hash power, they have, in turn, also taken control of more of the network. They can now make themselves responsible for decisions such as if and when to create a hard fork.

Ethereum, on the other hand, was created by known people and organizations: initially Vitalik Buterin, Anthony Di Iorio, Charles Hoskinson, Mihai Alisie, and Amir Chetrit. Joseph Lubin, Gavin Wood, and Jeffrey Wilke joined the project as founders shortly thereafter, and the founders eventually formed the Swiss-based Ethereum Foundation to oversee development.

The Ethereum DAO, built atop Ethereum, consisted of its investors. The more you invested, the more of a say or vote you received. This meant that The DAO had as many similarities to as differences from a normal, publicly traded corporation.

The story of The DAO, however, is one not of a community's rise and fall, but of its rise, fall, and resurrection. In July 2016, Ethereum took action to recover the hacked funds. The DAO voted—or rather 89 percent of The DAO "community" voted—for a hard fork or creation of a second blockchain, split off from the first. The second blockchain, also called Ethereum, issued a denial of the hacked transactions in the first blockchain, thereafter known as Ethereum Classic, returning the hacked funds to the investors who were members of The DAO community.

Clever as this maneuver was, it raised as many questions as it answered and created as many problems as it solved. Is a system you can fork when funds get tied up really decentralized?

The SEC certainly didn't think so. A year later, in July 2017, it issued a report declaring that The DAO, and tokens offered by similar "virtual organizations," were in fact securities subject to regulatory oversight. After the report was released, things got really crazy. Before any real crackdowns could occur, there was a proliferation of ICOs or "initial coin offerings." Different cryptocurrency "communities"—apologies for the many inevitable "scare quotes" in this chapter—were raising money through so-called utility tokens: the equivalent of preselling a membership to a club, such as a golf club, that doesn't yet exist.

The DAO was a monumental turning point in the still-early history of blockchain-based cryptocurrency. The SEC decided to set a precedent, and there is no question that The DAO came under scrutiny because it was perceived as being essentially an investor-directed venture-capital fund. Although there were as many differences as similarities, The DAO was clearly raising money to invest in other companies, a mission quite different from that which Satoshi Nakamoto's original cryptocurrency white paper set forth.

Another problem arose as these events unfolded. As members of the distributed autonomous organization, The DAO token holders were expected to vote on hundreds of investment proposals. Did every token holder have the time to review and properly critique all these proposals? Did they have the knowledge or expertise?

I don't think they did. I know that I, for one, didn't. After an investigation that included a thorough analysis of the charter, I concluded that this so-called decentralized autonomous organization was neither decentralized nor autonomous, but basically a rewrite of a traditional organizational structure, although one that a virtual community had significantly automated. Nevertheless, it still required a lot of human governance and centralization.

In my opinion, we're still a long way from being able to create fully decentralized organizations. Human nature is complex and has other tendencies than the desire to form and join communities with like-minded individuals. Given the history of The DAO, genuine community building would seem to involve more than the intersection of new digital technology and novel financial incentives. It requires governance.

The issue here is not whether the technology works or not. The technology behind decentralized autonomous organizations has already been created and proven. Rather, the underlying issues behind the viability of DAOs are economic, social, and political.

THE DEVELOPMENT CYCLE

There is a chicken-and-egg aspect to community building, governance, and the emergence of any widely adopted new technology. In technology, which came first: the infrastructure or its applications? The natural response is to say an infrastructure needs to be set up and established before applications can be built out. But the process is far more iterative and not nearly as linear as it seems.

The classic example is the light bulb, which was invented before the electric grid was put in place. The electric grid wasn't necessary to light up a light bulb: electricity could be generated locally. However, it was necessary to build electric grids before broader consumer adoption of light bulbs was possible. Broad consumer adoption then led to a profusion of new and different kinds of light bulbs.

Similarly, airplanes were invented before airports, but airports were required before airplanes and air travel could be widely adopted. All evolutionary processes seem to follow the same pattern.

A more recent and perhaps more relevant example is the internet itself. Basic internet protocols like TCP/IP were in place before the internet was widely adopted by the general public. During the technology's evolution, there was a mutually reinforcing feedback loop between its infrastructural and application layers. Once the web browsers that made it possible for the average person to use the internet arrived, setting off a series of competitive "browser wars," new consumer applications were proposed that required further infrastructural development before becoming truly viable. Internet service providers led to web portals, which led to search engines and then e-commerce applications like Amazon.

We're still very early in the blockchain development

cycle. New applications will be built that require further infrastructure and protocol development. These iterative cycles will continue to move exponentially in an upward trajectory, but there will be losers as well as winners, and many "learning experiences" on this evolutionary journey.

Since this is an iterative process, we really have no idea how it is going to develop. The "fortune tellers" who claim to know are just that. No one can predict the future. All I hope to achieve with this book is to help you recognize what we *don't* and *can't* yet know. We need to reframe the way we think.

Twenty years ago, who could have fathomed, much less predicted, what Google, Facebook, and Amazon would become? In 1999, if you had asked the MapQuest folks what their customers wanted, they would have said a better map. No one could have predicted that, in 2005, with the launch of Google Maps and their open approach to an API for sharing real-time location data, we would see the rise of an entire generation of unicorn tech companies: Uber, Lyft, Yelp, Airbnb, Delivery.com, Grubhub—the list goes on. The paradigm shift that enabled people to see a map as dynamic rather than static ushered in the entire "on-demand" economy.

We're at an analogous place today with blockchain. At the

moment, there is confusion about which developments belong in the infrastructure and which in the application categories. The point is that these categories, while important, are far from hard-and-fast. Bitcoin fundamentalists believe that the bitcoin application and its blockchain infrastructure are joined at the hip: bitcoin *is* an infrastructure. Given what happened with The DAO and subsequent ICOs, it's hard not to sympathize with this perspective, but that doesn't mean it's the end of the story.

A lot of ICO fundraising vehicles were malicious, and the SEC quite appropriately stepped in to weed them out. On the other hand, The DAO and its successors were also a new model of raising capital fundamentally different, in important respects, from the existing system. What will it evolve into? And how does it intersect with the many other currently emerging technologies?

THE FOURTH INDUSTRIAL REVOLUTION

It's critical to recognize that blockchain and cryptocurrency are part—an essential part—of the greater seismic sociocultural, geopolitical, economic, and technological shifts now taking place. Often referred to as the Fourth Industrial Revolution, this shift encompasses advances in machine learning and artificial intelligence, augmented and virtual reality, additive manufacturing, the Internet of Things, robotics, and genomics. The convergence of these technologies will impact the future of production, work, community, commerce, and everything in between. It's impossible to understand what's happening by reducing the interactions among all these technologies to a simple, two-dimensional map. What's occurring is multidimensional and therefore hard to fathom.

ORDERING PIZZA

... ON BLOCKCHAIN

... ON BLOCKCHAIN AND AI

... ON BLOCKCHAIN, AI, MZM

... ON BLOCKCHAIN, AI, MZM, GENETICS

This unique historical moment represents the convergence not just of multiple technologies, but of new ideas. Our thinking will shift from centralized to decentralized, opaque to transparent, siloed to open, reactive to proactive, and regulated to self-enforcing.

When I look at the greater evolution of thought taking place at the current moment, a term like "Fourth Industrial Revolution" doesn't seem to do this seismic paradigm shift justice. Perhaps the last time in human history we saw so significant a shift was the Paleolithic revolution, when humans took the evolutionary step of making and wielding tools. All subsequent revolutions, from the agrarian to the industrial to the internet revolution, represent accelerations of existing tool making.

The revolution we are now experiencing represents an evolution of thought and therefore requires us to conceive of and build new tools. If you don't buy that blockchain, as a technology, will be *the* backbone of this change, at least try to understand that it is a manifestation of a much larger evolutionary sociocultural process.

What will the next infrastructure-application matrix—the next light-bulb-and-energy-grid feedback loop—consist of? My sense is that what will emerge will include not only specific solutions or applications, but new ways of doing business and making transactions, along with new organizational and governance models.

This could have implications for voting and government, even including the demise of the concept of the nation-state, which our globalized and connected context seems to have rendered outdated. We just don't know, except that we do know fundamental transformation will take place at many different levels. Given what we've already seen in the multiple rises and collapses of various cryptocurrencies and blockchain networks, it's going to be a wild ride.

{ CHAPTER 5 }

BUILDING THE TRUSTLESS ECONOMY

In a recent survey of Gen Z, less than a tenth of the cohort who will constitute 40 percent of all US consumers by 2020 responded that they trust governments and corporations. A large majority of respondents are deleting some or all of their social media accounts.

We live in a world where trust has been eroded and continues to erode. The need for and potential of blockchain in such a world hit me viscerally when I first moved to the city by the bay.

WELCOME TO SAN FRANCISCO

In 2014, early in the history of blockchain, I moved to San Francisco to help start a company whose mission was to use the technology to secure non-financial assets like art, jewelry, land titles, and ownership records. I was a pioneer in a company using a technology whose implications I still didn't quite understand. At the time, I was standing in the same shoes as many of you reading this book are still standing in.

I moved into an apartment that was in one of the few new buildings that the city had allowed to be built. You entered the apartment by swiping an NFC (near field communications) card, like in a hotel, rather than a key.

I was so busy I really hadn't had time to unpack. After work one day, there was a knock on my door. It was a police officer, who asked, "Ma'am, are you missing anything?" It seems there had been seven robberies in the building. There were half-unpacked boxes all over my apartment, and the only thing I could answer was, "I don't know."

I quickly unpacked, went through my stuff, and realized my passport, credit card, checkbook, and all my jewelry were missing. The jewelry was mainly heirlooms from my grandparents. Both had passed away within a month of each other just a short while before. I hadn't insured it yet, and everything was gone. The emotional blow was worse than the financial one.

I realized that I didn't have any records of what I owned,

so I didn't really know exactly what was missing. In dealing with insurance, which is difficult enough to begin with, I had no proof of ownership or the jewelry's fair market value.

This wasn't breaking and entering. Obviously, someone had gotten into my and the other apartments using an NFC card. They had scanned in. However, I couldn't even get access to the records of who had entered my own apartment. It was written into the lease that only the building-management company could access these records. We had to get a warrant to see them.

Clearly, someone had been falsifying key cards in the leasing office. Whoever it was then went unchecked, entering different apartments over a number of months.

This was a turning point for me. I was going through all the difficulties of trying to build an early-stage business as well as the upset that the heirlooms my grandparents had given me were now gone. Then I realized how ridiculous it was that I didn't own or even have access to my own data.

Something clicked. Now I knew viscerally what the company I was starting was really all about. Renters, consumers, bank customers, and citizens have no access to their own data and information except through intermediaries, and it's impossible to be sure if those intermediaries can be trusted.

IN BLOCKCHAIN WE TRUST

That was the first time I realized the power of blockchain and its mission of granting or restoring self-sovereignty. We live in a world where we lack access, information, and trust. We don't trust our governments or the democratic process. Who could have foreseen that Facebook, a benign social network, could influence elections? We no longer trust the "fake news" in our media, the financial system responsible for the 2008 crisis, or brands whose products, touted by celebrities such as Jessica Alba and Gwyneth Paltrow, have been subject to recall.

What trust can blockchain actually provide, and how? This isn't a simple question with a simple answer, because trust, security, and privacy have many different meanings and manifestations, especially today when the security of our personal information, even our identities, feels at risk.

The point is often made that, though many of the web applications we use most often and find most useful are available at no apparent cost, it's because we are really paying with data about ourselves: who we are, what we do, what we buy, our likes and dislikes, our beliefs, and our political and social affiliations. We pay with our privacy.

In the past, trust was built in local communities, and exchange and communication were both localized. You trusted the people you knew and the community you were part of. You trusted that the products you purchased were safe and of high quality because you knew and trusted the person who made them. Of course, this localized "operating system" also had challenges: what you could access was limited. Everything was smaller in scope.

Then came the rise of industrialization, globalization, economies of scale, huge supply chains, and vast communications networks. We're now supposed to place trust in institutions like governments, banks, auditors, and brands. Communication is, also, now instant and global.

But what are the associated costs? Can we truly trust these intermediaries? In fact, the current operating system has created ever-widening trust gaps. As we rely more and more on centralized institutions, we forfeit more of our liberty, privacy, and security. Distrust has proliferated, and we have become skeptical of our institutions, governments, and financial systems. Having lost localized community connections, we have begun to distrust each other, our environment, and even ourselves.

As we transition into the operating system of the future, which will consist of a set of compacts and protocols that are social as well as technological, we are beginning to accept that trust and "security" in a globalized context can't be achieved through intermediaries. We require a new operating system that doesn't demand trust: a trustless system.

Blockchain, distributed ledger technology, or, more broadly, decentralization, aim to create just that: a trustless system that relies on properly designed and aligned incentives to facilitate peer-to-peer exchange in a global context. Only by no longer relying on trust will the operating system of the future usher in a new era of what it means to be and feel secure.

Previous chapters have touched on aspects of the blockchain technology that keep our transactions secure: accurate, unalterable, private, and untraceable. Such security is relative, as absolute security, whatever that might mean, is an ideal, which means, in the final analysis, that it's also an impossibility. In this chapter, we'll return to these aspects of blockchain security in greater depth while also broadening our scope.

WHAT IS THE PRICE OF TRUST?

The high-level question is why a decentralized blockchain ecosystem would provide greater security than centralized systems such as banks, government agencies, social media, and retail networks. These are all intermediaries that harvest and manage your data, often, as in the case of banks, charging you a fee to do so. Google and Facebook have become five-hundred-pound gorillas that control a large percentage of what you can access on the web.

Take Google, which started small, as the first really effective search engine, but has grown in less than twenty years into a dominant force in most of our lives. Google not only harvests the data you supply while using the search engine, but also when using applications like Gmail, which is now the most popular email system, the Chrome web browser, and the Android smartphone operating system.

Whether we're aware of it or not, we've put a lot of trust in these centralized intermediaries. We trust them to protect our information against hacking, and we also trust them to do the right things with our data. However, hacks haven't and won't stop, and both Facebook and Google are, at this writing, under investigation for misuse of and allowing unwarranted access to the data we have entrusted to them. The problem is that the average user has very little access to alternatives at present.

Financial institutions such as banks are similarly positioned with respect to our money, or rather the digital code, the 0s and 1s that represent our assets, credit, and debit data. Once I deposit my paycheck in my bank account, are the funds really "mine"? You may feel they are relatively secure and may be earning a bit of interest on them, but this is nothing in comparison to the interest the bank earns when it loans your and a lot of other people's money out to third parties, including yourself, who need more cash than they have on hand to buy a house, or car, or to start a company.

All this led to the financial crisis of 2008, in which the banks lost a lot of people's supposedly secure savings, but were themselves seen as "too big to fail." Frankly, even if you've stashed a wad of cash under your mattress, its value isn't necessarily stable. It certainly hasn't been if you live in a country like Greece or Venezuela.

Cryptographers and computer scientists began proposing some of the concepts behind cryptocurrency in the 1960s. Bitcoin put these concepts together at a unique moment in time: a major financial crisis. Shaken, people started waking up to the problems of security in a system controlled and largely created by huge intermediary organizations such as banks.

The idea behind cryptocurrencies was to stabilize and maintain value when it is transferred across geographic, political, or national borders. What excites cryptocurrency communities most is the ability to create relatively stable economic ecosystems in places where there is economic or political instability, such as, again, Greece or Venezuela. Money has been pouring into the local bitcoin markets in these countries.

Blockchain is meant to assure an even more fundamental sense of security: personal security and control. This is security in an almost libertarian sense, where ceding trust is seen as giving control to a centralized organization that can then exert control over you, even when such control can threaten your security and even identity. The use cases here extend far beyond cryptocurrency into such areas as health and genome records, deeds of title for land ownership, and even documents that prove who you are, such as birth certificates, driver's licenses, and passports.

TRUST AND PROOF

Then there is the technical aspect of blockchain security, which has been touched on before. Why is blockchain secure? Every block or transaction is recorded on the distributed ledger or blockchain. Once recorded on the blockchain, the transaction can't be altered, since an attempt to change it in one location would send an immediate signal that tampering was being attempted. You don't need to trust a blockchain record, because it's part of a system that doesn't require trust.

Also, as we've seen, before being recorded in a blockchain, a transaction or block must be cryptographically verified by one of a series of consensus algorithms. In the case of bitcoin and many other cryptocurrencies, such verification takes the form of "proof of work," where miners—computers on the network—all compete to solve an algorithm that validates that a unique, permissible transaction has been made. Those who solve the puzzle are rewarded with bitcoin or whatever cryptocurrency is being traded on their network.

This gets very technical, so let's simplify. (There is plenty of reference material out there on proof of work if you're technically inclined and interested.) Each block that is meant to be added to a blockchain is first encrypted by a process called secure hashing algorithm 256 (SHA-256). This converts the input into an encrypted string ("hash") of 256 characters. In order to be inserted into the block-chain, the hash in the current block needs to incorporate or point to the hash in the previous block. To simplify again, proof of work does not involve unhashing (decrypting) the data, but solving a puzzle involving the previous block's hash.

While there are other means of verifying blockchain transactions, such as proof of stake, proof of authority, proof of weight, and a crazy range of other consensus algorithms we won't get into, proof of work is the "OG" (original gangster) consensus algorithm, the most proven and therefore, at this point, still the most secure. It's been used in the bitcoin system for over ten years and has not encountered any problems or issues. It is difficult to compromise. In fact, the only way to hack the system would be for over 50 percent of the network of miners to mount an attack. While conceivable, this would be incredibly difficult because of the system's decentralization, which makes getting 51 percent of the miners responsible for verification to agree to an attack close to impossible.

The algorithm that miners are attempting to solve for involves a number with sixty-four hexadecimal digits. A hexadecimal digit is a digit that has a base of sixteen rather than a base of ten, meaning that the digit has a length of 16^{64}, which is almost impossibly huge. Only very advanced computers with a great deal of processing power can be used to mine cryptocurrency blocks.

A corollary of this is that bitcoin and other cryptocurrency mining uses a lot of power. This wasn't as true in the early days, when my brother was mining bitcoin on his gaming rig, but the system has grown considerably since then, and the hash power required to mine bitcoin has grown accordingly.

As mentioned earlier, a Chinese company called Bitmain was founded in 2013 to take advantage of China's relatively inexpensive coal-generated power. It has created the world's largest cryptocurrency mining farms with extremely powerful computers called ASICs—application-specific integrated circuits—that it designs and manufactures itself. These are regularly replaced with new computers with still more powerful processors. Bitmain then sells the used, less powerful ASICs to competitors who want to mine, but still won't be able to provide any real competition.

Bitmain's apparent attempt to establish a virtual monopoly on bitcoin-mining hardware ran into two major obstacles in 2018. The Chinese government, which had appeared to have encouraged the company's access to cheap power, decided early in the year that its energy supply could be better directed elsewhere. Bitmain also supported a hard fork of bitcoin that created a new cryptocurrency called Bitcoin Cash. A lawsuit was then filed against the instigators of the Bitcoin Cash hard fork, including Bitmain.

Proof of stake is an alternative, far less energy-intensive security strategy first proposed by Ethereum. Proof of stake basically verifies a block through a process of consensus among those who are already invested in the blockchain. Ethereum actually launched with a proof-of-work system, deciding that their version of proof of stake was insufficiently secure. That is, while Ethereum originally proposed proof of stake, it has yet to implement it.

Issues associated with proof of stake have led to proposals for refining and improving the methodology. One cryptocurrency, Decred, uses a hybrid proof-of-work/proof-of-stake system that it believes combines the best of both worlds, providing a higher level of security than stand-alone proof-of-stake systems while moderating the enormous energy demands a stand-alone proof-of-work system creates.

In proof-of-stake consensus, community members validate transactions. Stakeholders themselves are not personally asked or required to vote. Rather, the system runs a consensus algorithm that assigns voting privileges on a case-by-case basis to certain community members' computers.

Aside from proof of work and proof of stake, there are several other existing or proposed consensus algorithms that are still mainly speculative.

Proof of work is a core proposition of the bitcoin white paper and is still perceived as the most secure method of validating blockchain transactions. Other algorithms are more commonly used in permissioned or enterprise blockchains. Miners aren't validating these blockchains' code, as that would be extremely inefficient.

ZERO-KNOWLEDGE PROOF

Another more recently developed security methodology that is becoming more common is known as "zero-knowledge proof." There are many types of such proofs, one of the most prominent being zkSNARK, which stands for "zero-knowledge succinct non-interactive argument of knowledge." The mathematics behind this methodology is so complicated—far beyond hash cryptography—that even Ethereum co-founder Vitalik Buterin calls it "moon math." Instead of getting into the mathematical details, let's take a higher-level look at what zkSNARK was designed to do and how this relates to blockchain.

Basically, a zero-knowledge proof is a way for one party to prove to another party that they know a secret piece of information, such as a password, without having to reveal the information itself.

Let's say Bob wants to get into a bar in a state where the age limit for consuming alcohol is twenty-one. Of course, the simplest thing would be for him to show the bouncer his driver's license with his date of birth on it. But what if he doesn't want to reveal his date of birth or actual age, just that he is in fact twenty-one or older?

In that case, Bob would have to have a blockchain-based zero-knowledge-based ID card. The bouncer would scan the card to determine if Bob fits the age criteria for getting into the bar, without learning Bob's actual age. All the bouncer will learn is either yes, Bob meets the requirement, or no, he does not.

This is a trivial, if intriguing, example that has much greater applicability. One of the most popular cryptocurrencies, Zcash, uses zkSNARK to substantiate the validity of transactions without revealing—that is, while keeping secure—the details of the transactions themselves. The approach, despite the underlying mathematical complexity, turns out to be much more computationally efficient than proof-of-work. Once again, trust is not required!

The zkSNARK methodology has wide applicability in both public and permissioned enterprise blockchains, such as the one my company Chronicled launched for the pharmaceutical industry. Pharmaceutical drugs are placed in containers with serial numbers that are then shipped globally. In this case, zkSNARK technology can be used to prove that a certain batch of pharmaceuticals with a specific serial number has been shipped from one party to another, without revealing the actual serial numbers or any of the other specifics of the transaction, such as the name or amount of the drug being shipped.

To return to Bob: if he has a certain medical condition requiring that he take a certain drug, zkSNARK technology can confirm both facts without revealing the details of either the condition or the drug. If, rather than wanting to get into a bar, Bob is traveling to a foreign country, a "smart" passport could verify that he is a citizen of another country, such as the United States, allowed to travel there, without actually revealing the fact that he is an American citizen. There are many types of data, such as sensitive information about your genotype, where privacy is a real and far-from-trivial concern.

Again, the underlying issues here are privacy, security, and the need to verify without having to trust. These methods allow peer-to-peer transactions to be made without revealing the details of the transactions even to the parties themselves, much less to third parties such as banks and governments. The objection has been made that this could be done with criminal intent, but the same is true with many advances in technology. The security of certain types of data is critically important, and these are ways of ensuring privacy in an environment where trust has become an increasingly rare commodity.

PART II

CRYPTOCURRENCY AND CRYPTOGRAPHY

{ CHAPTER 6 }

IT'S ALL IN THE GAME

People find their way into cryptocurrency or blockchain through many different routes. Today, people hear about bitcoin from a friend, coworker, mainstream media, Uber driver—bubble alert!—or someone in finance. These people, in turn, found out about it from an acquaintance who might have been in the early gaming community, did bitcoin mining in college, or heard about trading coins from their sketchy cousin Paul, who made "millions" on day trading ICO "sh*tcoins." (More on these later.)

However, I believe that a lot of people who were into bitcoin at the very beginning, before 2011, came from a gaming background. They spent a lot of time on computers, like Alienware hardware, with a lot of processing power and powerful graphics cards. These computers had enough juice to do bitcoin proof-of-work mining, at least in the early days. Many gamers also spent a lot of time in chat rooms or on Reddit boards, where they were the first to hear about the latest advances. They were very much into experimenting with new technology.

BRIDGING THE PHYSICAL AND DIGITAL

I grew up exposed to gaming. I have two brothers, and one Christmas we all got Alienware computers. (Thanks, Mom and Dad!) We set up a little gaming zone in our basement, until our parents got upset with us for spending too much time online and sent us outside to play. (But why give us expensive gaming rigs if you're just going to kick us off?) I played a lot of early massively multiplayer online role-playing games (MMORPGs).

Some games involve collecting and trading things, others are adventure games, and still others are "first-person shooters." The ones that most interested me involved communities of players. I was very competitive on one of these games, *Tribes 2*. I would spend Saturday mornings competing to join a *Tribes 2* clan, which was basically a team. This is the sort of thing that has now evolved into esports: there are now massive esports teams whose fan base is larger than those of professional football teams.

I competed to get and was eventually accepted into a *Tribes 2* clan called {Spawl}. I had to meet up and practice with other members of my team before competing against others.

Many role-playing games involve advancing through and up different levels. You need to obtain or build tools to "level up." The game becomes an entire world in which you create or acquire virtual assets that are valuable within the game context, whether it's a power pack, a weapon like a sword, a healing juice or ointment, or whatever. Some of the earliest games that involved such virtual assets were *World of Warcraft* and *StarCraft*.

Anthropology was one of the focuses of my multidisciplinary major in college. For my thesis, I wanted to study not a real-world, but a virtual community with all or most of the aspects of a physical culture. At the time, social networks were still somewhat ambiguous, and the chair of the anthropology department thought I was a total nutcase. However, I convinced the department to allow me to live in and do an ethnographic study of a virtual world called Second Life.

Players or inhabitants in virtual worlds like Second Life create avatars of themselves. Having my own avatar meant I was able to follow the standard ethnographic methodology of being a "participant observer": simultaneously participating in and observing and studying a community or culture. My avatar, Shamwow Oximoxi—named affectionately after the late-night OxiClean infomercials with Billy Mays that I would watch while awake in the wee hours—lived "in-game" in the virtual world for six months while I was doing research. What I found most fascinating in the research was the ability to bridge the digital and physical worlds.

In Second Life, for example, you could build a virtual business. I created a T-shirt shop, Shamwow Shirts, designing digital T-shirts and selling them to other avatars. These T-shirts were entirely virtual, but had real value to the participants in the community, or ecosystem.

The process was fascinating, even though things were a lot more basic then. There was a chat interface—a

command-line interface, or CLI—you typed into. Micro-
phones you could talk into were added later. Now, games
incorporate virtual reality and goggles that put you all
the way inside the virtual world. In general, the distinction between the virtual or digital on the one hand and
the physical on the other is blurring, especially given the
amount of time most of us spend on our computers.

Second Life had an in-world currency called the Linden
dollar, named after Linden Labs, the studio that created
the game. Linden dollars had value in the community's
closed ecosystem. Other avatars could use them to buy
my virtual T-shirts. Even better, there were exchanges
where I could trade the Linden dollars I had been paid
for my T-shirts for actual US dollars. I could make "real"
money to compensate for the time I had spent designing
digital T-shirts to be worn in a digital world!

This was astounding, and it was exciting for me, as an
anthropologist, to wrap my head around an economic
exchange taking place both within and beyond a closed-
loop ecosystem. In Anthropology 101, there is an overused,
somewhat clichéd example of the Trobriand Islanders of
Papua New Guinea, who use shells as a means of transferring value: paper money is worthless among them.

However, this all bears on the critical issue of the social
aspects of how value and means of exchange are devel-

oped. We see this throughout history: tea bricks in nineteenth- and twentieth-century China, Mongolia, and Tibet; rai stones in Micronesia from AD 500 to the present; and Parmigiano-Reggiano wheels used as cash in northern Italy from about 1950 until now. Cheese money? You better believe it! How else do you expect me to make that Pizza I promised you?

It's easy to see the link between how something like Linden dollars worked and how bitcoin and other cryptocurrency tokens later came to operate. The behaviors that have developed around cryptocurrency have their origin in the gaming world.

While I was essentially doing "academic research," other players were making real-world profits. Brock Pierce started out as a child actor in Disney's *The Mighty Ducks* and got involved in gaming, particularly *World of Warcraft*, which, although not a virtual world like Second Life, was a massive multiplayer online role-playing game. People who played *World of Warcraft* or similar games, like *StarCraft*, my brothers' favorite, spent much of their time online. The game became the focus of their social life and interactions, and part of the play was collecting and trading in-game objects.

Brock Pierce then became a businessman heavily involved in creating currency-selling services for the virtual economies of these multiplayer games. Again, these were exchanges where players could sell in-game assets for "real money" on eBay or online forums. With the profits from this business, he and two partners established a venture capital firm called Blockchain Capital, which launched a cryptocurrency called EOS. Although his business dealings and life have been mired in controversy, Pierce's net worth is now estimated at $1 billion, and *Forbes* named him one of the twenty wealthiest people in crypto in 2018.

Pierce's story is an object lesson in the relationship between gaming and cryptocurrency. Cryptocurrency, like the Trobriand Islanders' shells, is a medium of exchange, and ledgers show up wherever value is exchanged, which is again where blockchain technology comes in.

Another related real-world context for exchange of all kinds is supply chains. *World of Warcraft* in-game assets and large-scale international supply chains may seem to be apples and oranges, but they have as many similarities as differences. Supply-chain permissioned blockchains, which we'll look at more closely in a later chapter, are now exploiting those similarities.

THE ART OF CRYPTO

Once it started taking off, cryptocurrency spread quickly, as might be expected, through the New York financial industry. What happened when and who influenced whom soon become complicated. Lines of transmission turn back on one another and become spiraling feedback loops.

There is a lot of graphical and literary or storytelling artistry in online gaming, so it seems almost inevitable that a group of crypto-focused artists would arise to use the technology to make art, some of which incorporates social critiques. As previously mentioned, there has even been some speculation that Satoshi Nakamoto is the English street artist Banksy. The chances of this being true are just about nil, but the rumor does reflect the artistic side of cryptocurrency, which, though very real, often goes unnoted.

Those of you in my generation, who came of age in the 1990s and 2000s, will remember Pokémon cards. These are playing cards—there is game-play involved—collectibles, and little works of art, all at the same time. Magic the Gathering cards were quite similar. Like baseball cards, these cards are non-fungible, which means that, while they can be traded and bought and sold, they don't have a predetermined cost—much like, as any gallery will tell you, a "real" work of art.

In October 2017, CryptoKitties, the first mainstream crypto-collectible, was created on the Ethereum blockchain. CryptoKitties could be bought, sold, and bred. Their purpose was originally more recreational than financial: blockchain, which had emerged in part from the gaming world, had become the backbone of new virtual games. Like rare Pokémon and Magic the Gathering cards, some CryptoKitties became quite valuable.

In the wake of this success, Ethereum created a new protocol, Ethereum Request for Comment-721 (ERC-721), which was developed as a means of creating digital collectibles and other non-fungible collectibles (NFCs) and tokens. This has spawned countless NFC-based games, which, while more complex, resemble CryptoKitties. Examples include *World of Ether*, where you don't merely breed collectible "monsters," but have them battle one another, and Blockade Games, a studio that has created *Plasma Bears* and *Neon District*, which enables many different kinds of complex interactions and adventures. All this may seem a long way from the kind of transactions that blockchain-distributed ledgers were developed to facilitate, but their emergence, if you think about it, is unsurprising.

The world of online gaming continues to evolve, as shown by the recent breakout success of Epic Games' *Fortnite*. The stereotype of a gamer as a loner without friends, usually sitting by herself in a basement, has been completely disproven. Web connectivity has made gaming a highly social activity. Top *Fortnite* players like Ninja, the online name of Richard Blevins, have become celebrities, broadcasting their games at considerable profit over the streaming network Twitch.

Fortnite players are not "wasting time." The game is a virtual community where they're meeting up with their friends and talking about what's important to them. They may even use the virtual meeting space as a place to work on school projects or take another player on a middle school date.

GEN Z

As gamers in the millennial generation, such as myself, were instrumental in the emergence of cryptocurrency and blockchain, we can expect to see gamers in "Generation Z"—the cohort born between 1993 and 2014, who have been raised as digital natives—exert a disproportionate influence on the future development of these technologies.

There are numerous Twitter posts from parents asking, "What do your kids think about crypto?" One answer might be, "My eight-year-old asked us to install Samourai Wallet on her smartphone and demanded we pay for her chores in bitcoin."

A recent survey showed that more than 50 percent of the Gen Z cohort are or want to be involved in cryptocurrency.[1] Another survey suggests that 43 percent of millennial respondents trust cryptocurrency exchanges more than US stock exchanges.[2] Fully digital transactions not limited by current boundaries seem a natural fit for these generations.

Generation Z, and to some extent millennials, have grown up with the web, social media, and handheld devices. They have a completely device-mediated approach to life. They straddle the physical and digital worlds in a way no other generation has.

When millennials like myself were growing up, our teachers still told us, "Online sources are not real sources. You have to go to the library and cite a book." If I had taken my middle school teachers aside and told them that I would one day write a physical book in which I would cite Wikipedia pages, Twitter posts, blogs, podcasts, and Snapchat stories—just kidding about the Snapchat!—they probably would have had a fit and told me I was spreading blasphemy.

---

1   Shalin Soni, "Around 50% of American Gen Z on the Verge of Using Crypto Currencies: Survey," *CryptoNewsZ*, September 7, 2018, https://www.cryptonewsz.com/around-50-of-american-Gen Z-on-the-verge-of-using-crypto-currencies-survey/920/.

2   Jessica Klein, "Survey: Millennials Trust Nothing, Except Maybe Crypto," *BreakerMag*, February 19, 2019, https://breakermag.com/survey-millennials-trust-nothing-except-maybe-crypto/.

Back then, my teachers no doubt had a point when they said, "You can't trust anything on a web page." You've still got to be careful now in this time of crazy "fake news." However, many, if not most, web pages are relatively trustworthy, and few of us now balk at entering our credit card numbers on a web form, which was once thought to be dangerous. Caution is, of course, always warranted, but today's high schoolers are very tech enabled and comfortable with digital services. Their outlook is connected and globalized. They're able to communicate with people all over the world and have grown up with that expectation.

Gen Z and millennials have also seen the dark side of global connectivity and the trust gaps it causes. They've come of age in an era of fake news, recessions, and brands greenwashing their products, making baseless claims for marketing purposes. Given that Gen Z will make up 40 percent of all US consumers by 2020, it is imperative, if they want to remain competitive in this changing landscape, that companies invest in solutions that establish trust.

WHAT GOES AROUND

The overlap among art, gaming, and blockchain technology deserves more recognition than it has gotten. It's going to become increasingly important. Marguerite deCourcelle, better known as Coin Artist (@coin_artist), is co-founder of Blockade Games, which uses blockchain to build games that integrate puzzles and art. Her crypto-puzzle painting called *TORCHED H34R7S*, which integrated several thousand dollars in bitcoin, was finally unlocked after three years of attempts.

Blockade Games has expanded beyond puzzles to role-playing games (RPGs), such as *Neon District*, created in decentralized fashion through blockchain technology. Players can join in creating the games or not, just as they choose. The studio is embracing the ethos of decentralization while simultaneously driving user adoption and education. The resulting games often combine entertainment and storytelling with encryption and puzzle solving.

In these projects, artists, gamers, and storytellers are all contributing to the creation of new worlds. What is the world's history or backstory? What kind of people live there? Collectively imagining future realities may well help manifest or create those realities, as has already been the case with cryptocurrency.

All this involves bringing people with different skillsets and capabilities together to shape constantly evolving, interactive stories. Many such projects have been influenced by the ever-popular Choose Your Own Adventure books. The first page of such a book might say, "If you want to go into the room, go to page three. If you are scared and want to turn away from the door, go to page sixty-three." You could read the book or play the game a hundred times, and each reading would take you on a different journey.

In this decentralized, collaborative environment, what you're building continues to grow through everyone's contributions. The story or narrative becomes global. It's a lot like building applications based on open-source code stored in a repository such as GitHub, where other members of your "work group" can look at, approve, and integrate what you've done into the master code base.

The creative spirit of the gaming world helped create cryptocurrency and blockchain technology, which is now returning the favor. A creative community gathers to build a game, an artwork, a narrative, or an alternative reality to which any member can make a contribution or "mod" (modification). Storytelling and realizing alternative realities have both become collaborative.

This all bears on the evolving future of work itself: what people do to create value and how they do it. The gaming world has enabled us to feel comfortable collaborating with people all over the world. We are seeing teams form, like organic ecosystems, on social media websites like Twitter or communications tools like Discord and Slack.

Some of the fastest-growing startups, like the design software Invision, are completely distributed, with team size upwards of six hundred people. Blockchain technology has and will continue to support and enable this trend. In time, the way products and services are created may well become much more like online gaming has been for some time.

{ CHAPTER 7 }

THE ZILLION-DOLLAR PIZZA: BITCOIN'S MYTHOLOGY AND EVOLVING VALUE(S)

Ah, yes, the moment you've been waiting for. Here comes the Pizza.

On May 22, 2010, programmer Laszlo Hanyecz made the first purchase of real-world goods with bitcoin: two Papa John's Pizzas. He structured the deal with a fellow member of the Bitcoin Talk forum, the online meeting place for bitcoin originalists.

He paid ten thousand bitcoin in exchange for the US dollars he bought the two Pizzas with. Bitcoin was worth only a few pennies apiece at the time, so the value of the transaction was twenty-five dollars for a total of sixteen slices. It was the first real-world bitcoin transaction, and boy did that Pizza taste good. Almost as good as the Pizza I will give you at the end of this book.

At one point, when bitcoin's value was particularly high, it was estimated that, at then-current rates, Laszlo had paid a little under $42 million for each Pizza, a total of $83.7 million for both. You can do the per-slice calculations yourself.

Now the community celebrates May 22 as Bitcoin Pizza Day. My favorite holiday, by far.

BETTING ON BITCOIN

The public is fascinated by the recurrent rise and fall of bitcoin's value. This is an understandable perspective on the first cryptocurrency, which was established as a disintermediated, distributed medium of exchange in large part in response to the 2008 financial crisis. It was also a response to a social and cultural, as well as monetary, crisis, since bitcoin's cultural aspects are, in my opinion, as significant as the financial ones.

From 2009 to 2013, bitcoin remained under a dollar. Then it suddenly became more valuable than gold. People's attention followed the money.

To me, an equally important takeaway is that the early

creators and users of bitcoin were alternative-minded people into gaming and some of the more fringe aspects of digital technology. Did these people, even the mysterious Satoshi Nakamoto her/him/them/itself, believe that bitcoin would become a global phenomenon? Perhaps not, although I'm not sure. Satoshi's original white paper was clearly meant to have wide applicability.

Can you have the foresight, in creating something like bitcoin, to know what it's actually going to become? Once innovations like Apple, Google, or Facebook start taking off, their growth can be purposely leveraged. Mark Zuckerberg certainly did everything he could to turn Facebook into a proverbial Silicon Valley unicorn. However, the history of digital technology is also littered with supposedly move-fast-and-break-things, can't-fail, get-rich-quick ideas that never went anywhere.

However, remember that bitcoin, unlike Facebook, was and remains leaderless. You might almost say "faceless." All we know for sure about Satoshi Nakamoto is that they put their name on a white paper that turned out to be extremely influential.

There is a consensus, or at least semi-consensus, opinion that no one really expected bitcoin would go so far mainstream, although that may have been some people's hope.

Bitcoin's alternative beginnings implied that it wasn't meant to go mainstream, almost by definition.

THE EMERGING CRYPTO CULTURE

All this has led to considerable controversy both inside and outside the ecosystem. We'll devote an entire chapter to "no-coiners": economists, investors, and others who criticize the entire concept of cryptocurrency, although a couple of battles royale will be mentioned here as a preview of coming attractions.

Nouriel Roubini, a professor at NYU's Stern School of Business, has been a very outspoken critic of cryptocurrency more than willing to employ shock-and-awe terminology. He has been both berating and blocking people on Twitter—one of the crypto community's main communications mediums—and testified in the Senate. He calls crypto a cesspool and those involved with it either idiots or criminals. One of Roubini's key targets is Ethereum co-founder Vitalik Buterin, who has not been taking the criticism lying down.

Debate and controversy also flourish within the crypto community itself. Jimmy Song, a bitcoin maximalist, has challenged Ethereum's Joe Lubin to take a bet that Ethereum would or would not hit a market cap by a certain date. The canny Lubin has not taken the bait, making no commitments or projections. As Nick Paumgarten's October 22, 2018, *New Yorker* article, "The Stuff Dreams Are Made Of," has related, there are those who hold in general that crypto "bets" are a myth. Of course, mythology, especially during the emergence of a new sociocultural phenomenon, can be as influential as so-called reality. Indeed, as we've seen, origin myths tend to create their own reality.

Bitcoin's countercultural beginnings may not be anarchistic per se. However, the impulse toward decentralization and disintermediating such intermediaries as the government and other large institutions was crucial to crypto's origins.

The thesis that blockchain is the operating system of the future is an expression of what I feel is a very real and ongoing paradigm shift that is still in its early stages. The shift has many different facets: from centralized to decentralized, opaque to transparent and trusted, siloed to connected, and regulated to self-enforcing.

These shifts from the current to a new paradigm could all be called countercultural in the broadest sense. I might go so far as to say this paradigm shift is "extracultural" or "supercultural," since we're transcending our current operating system and leveling up.

We tend to think of the term "counterculture" in sixties or

seventies terms—the hippies and Vietnam protests—but the term has greater applicability. Most of our cultural systems, whether they be financial, governmental, communications, or agricultural, are highly centralized. The "extracultural" systems we're now building are networked and peer-to-peer, bypassing and even eliminating the center.

Bitcoin and other cryptocurrencies are also extracultural in asserting, for instance, that we don't need banks and shouldn't trust them. We shouldn't have to pay a fee or have a wire transfer take five days to send money across borders, perhaps to family members in other countries. This stance challenges our deeply entrenched existing global systems and the current rules of the global economy.

Some of this may be paranoid, and many bitcoin maximalists are libertarian by nature. NYU's Nouriel Roubini's critique is in part an assertion that cryptos are wacky, right-wing gun-toters and that the crypto world is just nuts.

In my opinion, some of crypto's values, in fact, arise from an attempt to assure self-preservation, self-sovereignty, and privacy. However, crypto's underlying values are not solely self-centered, but also involve networks of individuals and everyone's right to participate in this global ecosystem.

This is in part a response to the 2008 financial crisis, which I bring up again because it truly is important to crypto and blockchain, but tends to be ignored or forgotten in current discussions of the technology. Trust banks and other financial institutions? They're the ones who came up with all these new-fangled derivatives, such as credit-default swaps and other complex financial products, which turned out to have no real foundation—talk about mythology!—and led to the mortgage crisis and the falling of the dominoes.

Trust government? It was the government that bailed out the financial institutions that created the financial crisis, because they were "too big to fail," while leaving individuals, not too big to fail, in the lurch. Of course, a reasonable argument might be made that government intervention was necessary to staunch further collapse. Satoshi Nakamoto, however, came up with an alternative proposal.

The year 2008 was the proverbial perfect storm. Everyone began feeling uneasy about both the American and world economies. Would a global financial collapse ensue, and, if so, what would it look like? On the other hand, many financial advisors said and still say, "That's ridiculous. That's never going to happen. This is like a doomsday conspiracy theory."

Saying something's a "conspiracy theory" is a time-honored way of dismissing it by calling it crazy. What this dismissal doesn't recognize is that crypto and blockchain are a social movement as well as a technology, and powerful social movements have a tendency to shift paradigms in often unpredictable ways.

This is how history is made, so it's important to focus on history. Certain moments in time give rise to new ideas, and ideas, like religions, can and do change history. They shift our perception, our ways of seeing and acting in the world.

BEYOND BORDERS

The shift isn't a simplistic one from pro-government and pro-regulation to anti-government and anti-regulation. Many crypto fundamentalists support government, or at least regulatory, scrutiny. However, a possibly complementary perspective is developing based on the realizations that (1) a nation-state is in many ways defined only by borders drawn on a map; (2) a corporation is just a legal definition; and (3) fiat currency is ultimately backed by military prowess and nuclear bombs.

There is also the clear recognition that many national governments are unstable and subject to sudden power shifts, making the attempt to create disintermediated, extra-governmental peer-to-peer networks anything but crazy. In fact, they're more sensible than many of the institutions that persist in our current globalized context.

The Soviet Union fell apart just recently, historically speaking. The Ottoman Empire, which had been in existence for seven hundred years, finally collapsed in 1922, less than a hundred years ago. The fallout continues in both cases. European colonial states, such as the United Kingdom and France, drew lines on paper dividing the landmass of the Ottoman Empire into such states as Syria, Iraq, and Iran. Ongoing instability among ethnic and cultural groups, and over access to vital resources such as oil, resulted and has continued in the region up to the present day. The breakup of the Soviet empire has had similar consequences.

While history itself is quite complicated, these examples point to the tension that results from the rise and fall of governments. The response—especially given that we live in an age where digital technology is transforming the world—is, in the case of crypto, an attempt to create a means of exchange whose value transcends geopolitical structures and boundaries. The motivating impulse is to provide a sense of security, particularly in places where political and financial insecurity have become the norm.

Cryptocurrency isn't anti-government in a frighteningly nihilistic way, as some have asserted. It's based on a real examination of a real question: can we still trust current civil structures? They've worked, more or less, relatively well for quite some time. However, given that the global economy is transforming, can these historical structures still be relied upon?

Ongoing crises such as those in the Greek and Venezuelan economies, as well as the Great Recession of 2008, would seem to give substance and credence to cryptocurrency's original mission of establishing financial power and security through peer-to-peer networks and, by extension, the people who make up those networks.

This is happening on a number of different fronts and scales. Many current crypto projects, which get little play in the American press, focus on "mesh networking," devices that enable bitcoin and other cryptocurrency transactions to take place where there is no or little access to cell phone service or internet service providers. The focus here is remote rural areas, such as in Colombia, whose inhabitants are already becoming well versed in this approach. Much of this is based on extremely localized small-scale communication.

Then, there's the much larger scale we usually focus on when considering cryptocurrency. A globally useful digital currency must be transacted internationally. The corresponding ethos is countercultural, not so much in a political sense, but because it runs counter to the centralization of internet service providers and cellular data networks entirely controlled and managed by huge communications corporations. Such centralization limits access and bandwidth and enables these corporations to charge exorbitant subscription and other fees.

THE POWERS THAT BE

Speaking of large corporations such as banks, there is tremendous controversy over Ripple, which was proclaimed the "cryptocurrency of 2017." The conflict again focuses on centralization versus decentralization. A large portion of the crypto community dislikes Ripple because Ripple Labs has entered into partnerships with international banks and other institutions that intend to use its tokens to facilitate financial exchanges.

Also, Ripple Labs, according to its critics, created and profited from Ripple's token, XRP, by means of centralization. Blockchain fundamentalists see Ripple tokens and the company that created them as a way to both make use of and subvert decentralizing blockchain technology in the service of centralization and intermediation.

This controversy can neither be fully explored nor resolved here. Both sides offer impassioned arguments. There is a lot of misapprehension and bickering, which is hardly a new phenomenon. At one point, President Trump offered his opinion that since China controls bitcoin—because of the one-time Chinese near-monopoly on proof-of-work mining—Ripple was a preferable alternative: "Hate bitcoin; love Ripple."

One size does not fit all. The controversy stems from the fact that crypto and blockchain technology can be used to meet different needs in different circumstances. If the goal is to empower people in unstable financial and political communities, some degree of centralization is clearly needed. If the goal is to uphold the existing financial system more efficiently—well, that runs counter to cryptocurrency's initial purposes and tendencies.

Given the speed of technological change, there's no doubt that large, powerful existing institutions are intent on retrofitting: using blockchain technology to make current processes faster and more efficient. No one, including crypto fundamentalists, is naïve enough to expect the powers that be to say, "Okay, cool, we're just going to give up everything and everyone that benefits from the existing system and move to a decentralized world."

Intermediaries make a lot of money. Banks and wholesale distributors in supply chains—the middlemen—are often the most profitable institutions in the systems they facilitate. Although they are less trusted than they were formerly, they are not going to give up power and suddenly assert, "You don't need me anymore. Let's facilitate global peer-to-peer communications and transactions in every possible respect, from mortgages to agriculture and food supply."

HARD FORKS

The concept of a "hard fork"—breaking off a new blockchain, with new requirements or parameters, from an old one—is ideological as well as technological. There is a fundamental ideological difference between believing in the importance of centralization in appropriate circumstances and using blockchain as a convenient buzzword or new technology to uphold an existing structure. However, many companies, including big players in the financial sector, are doing precisely this, sometimes simply by adding "blockchain" to their names for marketing purposes.

For example, Fidelity Investments is in the process of offering institutional financial products to enable customers to invest in crypto. They've recognized that they've got to get on the bandwagon and become involved. Of course, they're going to want their piece of the pie, so centralized transaction fees will definitely be involved.

The crypto community is hardly immune to self-serving

buzzwords either. Crypto fundamentalists are also human, all too human. Their hard forks, however, tend not to cross the ideological line between decentralization and centralization. Bitcoin hard forks have, for the most part, operated under a common belief in or ideology of a decentralized future. Most disagreements regarding bitcoin hard forks have tended to be more about implementation and technology.

The truth is that it can be hard to get to the heart of the matter in a lot of these disagreements. Bitcoin Cash was a hard fork from the original bitcoin that many, certainly many bitcoin fundamentalists, saw as a scam devised by the Chinese proof-of-work mining company Bitmain to cash in. While the details are obscure, what's important is to recognize that these controversies exist.

This is nothing new in world history. There's a wonderful chart that shows the global spread of world religions and how they broke up and separated like branches spreading from the trunk of a giant tree.[1]

---

1   Simon E. Davies, "The Evolutionary Tree of Religion," *Infographics Blog*, November 28, 2014, http://www.infographicsblog.com/the-evolutionary-tree-of-religion-simon-e-davies/.

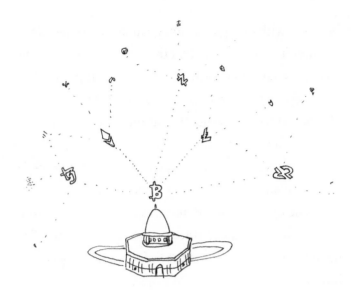

It would be great if there were a similar chart for crypto, although it probably wouldn't be possible to create one at this early stage in the technology's evolution.

Crypto forks aren't limited to bitcoin. The hack of The DAO (decentralized autonomous organization) created by Ethereum forked the code base into Ether, the new currency, and Ether Classic, the old, in order to recover the hacked funds. It achieved that goal cleverly, although crypto fundamentalists disagreed with the methodology employed—and with The DAO in general—because, despite the name, the process was considered and perhaps actually was centralized rather than decentralized.

Sia, a blockchain created as a way of decentralizing cloud

storage—with a cryptocurrency called Siacoin developed as a medium of exchange for these transactions—forked its code base to prevent two mining companies from creating a network monopoly. The two companies were Bitmain, the Chinese giant, and Innosilicon, which had just developed computers with an even faster application-specific integrated circuit (ASIC) specifically designed to mine Siacoin. This move divided the Sia ecosystem, some of whose members felt that it was wrong for the community to come together to block someone—anyone—from the network. They believe the fork centralized a network intended to be fundamentally open.

Monopolies, on the other hand, are by definition closed systems. Should a principle be sacrificed on one level in order to be maintained on another? The technology to prevent monopolies from forming does not seem to have been developed yet. It could also be argued that capitalism is so deeply ingrained in our current socioeconomic systems that monopolies are bound to arise.

THE DECENTRALIZATION PRINCIPLE

The purpose here is not to resolve these conflicts and controversies—if they can be resolved at all—but to show that they have arisen in the cryptocurrency sphere and will undoubtedly continue to arise. Limited growth or unlimited growth? Decentralization, centralization, or a compromise between the two?

Despite the splits and factions that have arisen, the original use case is and continues to be decentralization. It all comes down to a matter of degree and level of "purity," which is why I call the original bitcoin community "maximalists." These controversies, forks, and splits are bound to continue. Can security and privacy be best achieved in this way or that? In many cases, the answers are anything but clear and simple.

Again, the overarching principle is decentralization. In my opinion, where blockchain and cryptocurrency technologies are being utilized to promote centralization, they are no longer blockchain or crypto in any meaningful sense of the terms.

Of course, there are also "no-coiners," who feel the whole crypto movement is anything from unwise to criminal. We'll deal with their critiques in greater depth below. However, even or perhaps especially the staunchest crypto maximalists welcome no-coiner critiques. They understand you can't propose and implement anything—especially a financial system—completely outside the realm of reality. Healthy debate about ways and means should be encouraged.

Some way, somehow, a transition or bridge from the existing system to a new one will need to be built. While they may have a countercultural element, effective crypto and blockchain technologies can't be completely countercultural, ignoring the current context and starting from scratch. There is an existing system that needs to be considered and adjusted in the migration to less centralized processes.

CRYPTO LIFESTYLES

As long as we're on the subject, just who are these crypto people anyway? There are the:

- Maximalists, who believe bitcoin is *the* use case for blockchain
- HODLers, long-game investors "Holding On for Dear Life" through volatile markets
- OG ("original gangster") traders in the game from the beginning, who have seen at least three bitcoin bubbles: a drop from $31 back down to about $2 in 2011; a high of $1,242 in 2013 descending to a low of about $200 in 2015; and a precipitous descent from a top of $19,783.06 in 2017 that took place in only a month
- Institutional traders
- Developers and designers, working not just to HODL, but "BUIDL" or "Build for Dear Life"
- ICO scammers, who raised millions from unsuspecting retail investors

- Trolls, who post memes and negative comments on Twitter
- Shills promoting a certain coin or company, usually also on Twitter
- No-coiners
- InfoSec (information security and cybersecurity) techies
- "Crypto bros," who resemble tech bros and finance bros
- Ethereum community as a whole, quite eclectic in itself, whose members can often be seen at conferences with rainbows and unicorns on their T-shirts
- Bot armies that aren't even real people
- Thought leaders, journalists, podcasters, newsletter writers

And that's only just the beginning.

There's no way to do a "typical user profile," as these people are anything but typical. There are tons of archetypes in the community, but generalization is dangerous, although impossible to avoid.

As a trained pilot who has done hundreds of competitive skydives, I'm both typical and atypical, since on the one hand, I'm a risk-taker, and on the other, while believing in risks, I'm frankly afraid of heights. As an anthropologist, I'm almost as interested in the phenomenon's cultural and lifestyle elements as its potential financial and business impact. As an engineer, I'm interested in building and manifesting social systems through technology. Where do I fit? A female, risk-taking technical anthropologist who enjoys economics and can do some physics stuff? Screw fitting in!

GOING KETO

One of the most "liked" of my many blog posts on the subjects of crypto and blockchain was on the popularity of the keto diet among hard-core crypto adopters. The keto or ketogenic diet emphasizes eating fats and eliminating or greatly reducing carbohydrate intake, often to less than 5 percent of daily intake. Ketosis is a metabolic state in which the body burns fats rather than carbohydrates to produce energy. As opposed to most "dietary lifestyles," the keto diet consists largely of good fats like oils and avocados, red meat, fatty fish such as salmon, eggs, and dairy foods.

Like crypto, the keto diet is countercultural in that it flips things on their heads. The FDA food pyramid and other conventional dietary advice tell us to avoid fats and focus on vegetables and grains. Those who practice the keto diet counter that the standard recommended diet is evolutionarily unsound and the research behind it is biased.

The keto community is even more hard-core than the

prolific hip-hop group NWA—not only saying "F*ck tha Police," but also, "F*ck everything you knew or thought you knew about everything, including what the government tells you to eat, because they are all just trying to shill their grains." Regardless of what the FDA thinks, the keto diet is to a large extent the "Paleo" diet, meaning the diet eaten by our ancestors, placing emphasis on fresh foods and meats, encouraging our bodies to become fat adapted, meaning able to burn fat rather than carbohydrates for energy. Enthusiasts believe this is the diet best suited to our overall continued health.

A lot of crypto fundamentalists are keto "meatheads." This generates numerous bad puns, such as taking a "steak" rather than a "stake" in a cryptocurrency. I was intrigued by the keto diet and tried it myself for four months. When I was in ketosis, I found things were super sharp and that my body seemed to be functioning optimally. However, eating bacon and avocados all day, despite what you may think, does become difficult to keep up. I missed that Pizza.

IS PIZZA A MYTH?

The larger cultural and lifestyle observation is that many crypto community members are both bio-hackers and computer hackers. They tend to question everything, especially received wisdom from centralized organizations such as the FDA. Perhaps, they suggest, a conspiracy is involved, with the FDA touting grains simply because they are the mainstay of big agriculture.

The question "Do you eat keto?" appears frequently in communications among crypto fundamentalists. Originally, Reddit boards were the community's most common communications medium. Now it's Twitter. There's so much crypto tweeting that sometimes I don't know what else these people do all day. They seem to be spending most of their time tweeting, talking to, and fighting with one another.

This leads to some of the negative fallout we've come to expect from social networks. Scammers deploy bots that tweet phishing scams to people's accounts. One scam that spread so much like wildfire that it almost became a cultural joke were tweets with a photo of Vitalik Buterin of Ethereum with a fake, but plausible return address. The tweet read, "I'm doing an Ether giveaway. Click this link."

Of course, the scam was no joke to those who got taken in, including techies who should have known better. In 2017, it got so crazy that people were changing their Twitter names to "not giving away Eth" and the like, just to raise awareness of the scammers. Some major figures, such as Elon Musk, asked Jack Dorsey of Twitter to fight back and get rid of the phishing bots.

Above all, the blockchain and crypto community is rich: rich in its culture, diverse in its participants, a constantly evolving, living ecosystem. Like many communities of practice, there are common member archetypes and mediums of exchange. There are different clans, values, and belief systems. Different eating habits and clothing styles. There is no single individual, ecosystem, or myth that can define it all. Along with the myth of Satoshi Nakamoto, which tipped the domino that created this global social movement, Bitcoin Pizza Day represents the tipping point where a seemingly innocuous bitcoin-for-Pizza exchange became a bridge from the techie ambiguity of zeros and ones to the current culture.

Both myth and history function to promote power-sustaining ideologies by naturalizing, universalizing, and rendering them self-evident and inevitable. Myth, in its utter ambiguity and refusal to lay claim to truth, creates the illusion of reality. We are in a unique moment in human history where we are working together to shape not only new technologies, but new, binding myths. We are finally looking beyond the myths that shaped our past and that we took to be self-evident—myths like centralization, opacity, and silos—to get our first glimpse into a world that may have been there all along and will start defining our new reality.

{ CHAPTER 8 }

TOKENS: CRYPTOCURRENCY BEYOND BITCOIN

In the late 1980s, gas stations in remote areas of the Netherlands were struggling with a problem. Their cash was being robbed in the middle of the night. The stations had to stay open twenty-four hours to service trucks that needed refueling, but didn't want to invest in hiring guards for each location. What did they do? They loaded the cash onto a card and stopped getting robbed. Simple, right?

Fast-forward about fifteen years. As a teen, I borrowed my parents' car and used a gas card not only to fill up the tank, but to purchase a Visa gift card I then used to buy all sorts of fun things my parents didn't know about.

We've since seen the rise of numerous sophisticated point-of-sale systems. Starbucks' digital gift cards helped its app go viral among suburban women. There are loyalty-points programs, mobile payments, and everything in between.

Whether we know it or not, we've been dabbling in virtual and digital currencies for quite some time now. Bitcoin, nevertheless, was the first cryptocurrency—a means of creating and exchanging value, made possible by blockchain technology—to reach relatively mainstream success. Then along came Ethereum. The number and types of cryptocurrencies have continued to multiply throughout their still relatively short history, which, let's remember, only goes back to 2009.

SCALABILITY AND PROLIFERATION

Satoshi Nakamoto's original white paper mandated the creation, or "mining," of a maximum of twenty-one million bitcoins. The reason behind this limitation is a topic of debate. Some speculate that an arbitrary number was chosen to avoid flooding the market.

Others believe the amount was calculated mathematically. Bitcoin miners receive a fifty-bitcoin reward for every bitcoin block they mine. The reward is cut in half every 210,000 blocks. The smallest indivisible bitcoin unit (the bitcoin "penny") is called a Satoshi, which is one hundred millionth of a bitcoin (0.00000001 BTC).

Doing a complex calculation with this information gives a result of twenty-one million bitcoins.[1]

Others put forth celestial theories. The earth, spinning on its axis, completes one full rotation every twenty-four hours or 1,440 minutes. A new bitcoin block is created every 10 minutes, meaning 144 are created in a day. Coincidence?

In any event, by August 2018, seventeen million of the twenty-one million possible bitcoins had been mined. This limitation has imposed a bottleneck that means the currency isn't "scalable." This is a supply and infrastructure problem, since the expectation of exponential scalability is one of the holy grails of digital technology. The more people who use Facebook, the more valuable Facebook becomes.

This twenty-one million bitcoin limitation is one of the drivers behind the creation of other cryptocurrencies, as it was behind the many "soft" (backward-compatible) and "hard" (non-backward-compatible) forks in bitcoin itself. These forks have proliferated to such an extent that, as of late 2018, there were over 425 bitcoin varieties: Bitcoin Cash, Bitcoin Diamond, Bitcoin "Whatever."

---

1   In case you're interested in looking up the calculation, go to https://coinsavage.com/content/2018/11/the-21-million-bitcoin-story-explained-why-is-the-number-special/.

By late 2018, there were also already thousands of different cryptocurrencies, with the proliferation almost certain to continue, especially during crypto bull markets. Some of these non-bitcoin cryptocurrencies, such as Ether, have been mentioned already. There is controversy over whether Ripple, for instance, is a blockchain-based cryptocurrency at all or a centralized one. Other cryptocurrencies, such as Siacoin, have been created to facilitate transactions on special-purpose distributed networks, which in Sia's case involve cloud storage. Filecoin is another cryptocurrency developed to facilitate Protocol Labs' file-storage network, which competes with Sia.

Making a list and attempting to describe each of these cryptocurrencies would be, basically, impossible. They are proliferating, and an encyclopedic approach would provide little enlightenment. Let's focus on some major trends and inflection points instead.

ETHEREUM

The second major cryptocurrency, as we've seen, was Ether. In order to fund the development of the Ethereum project, which was founded to create a distributed application software platform, Ethereum's creators presold Ether, its token, during a 2014 crowdsale. In 2016, Ethereum created The DAO (decentralized autonomous organization) to raise funding for Ethereum projects.

Shortly after The DAO—which bitcoin fundamentalists view as neither decentralized nor autonomous—was created, it was hacked, a move countered by a hard fork that created a new cryptocurrency that came, confusingly, to be called Ether, in distinction to the original Ether, now called Ether Classic.

The differences between Ethereum and the bitcoin community are as instructive as the similarities. Both are key players in and originators of different approaches to cryptocurrency and blockchain. While bitcoin's Satoshi Nakamoto remains a mysterious figure, a number of non-anonymous, indeed vivid, personalities were responsible for the creation of Ethereum. The most prominent are Vitalik Buterin and Joe Lubin. It's hard not to see these two "founding fathers" as almost clichéd opposites. Vitalik, as he is known, represents the brilliant, idealistic tech nerd and Lubin the equally, but contrastingly brilliant Machiavellian businessman. Both grew up in Toronto, and for a time they formed a highly successful, if uneasy, alliance.

Vitalik, like bitcoin maximalists, comes from the alternative, countercultural side of the equation. He emigrated with his family from Chechnya to Canada at age six, having already started fooling around with computers, and became an avid gamer. Introduced to bitcoin early on, he began focusing on the unexplored possibilities of both crypto and blockchain technology.

On his personal website, Vitalik states:

> I happily played World of Warcraft during 2007–2010, but one day Blizzard removed the damage component from my beloved warlock's Siphon Life spell. I cried myself to sleep, and on that day I realized what horrors centralized services can bring. I soon decided to quit.

> In 2011, searching for a new purpose in life, I discovered Bitcoin. At first, I was skeptical, and did not understand how it could possibly have value without physical backing. But slowly I became more and more interested. I started writing for a blog called *Bitcoin Weekly* initially at a meek wage of $1.50 per hour, and soon with Mihai Alisie co-founded *Bitcoin Magazine*.[2]

Vitalik's Satoshi-esque white paper, which appeared in late 2013 and was written when he was only nineteen, proposed a "blockchain app platform," which is to say, a platform for building blockchain-enabled applications, also known as "smart contracts," a term that Nick Szabo, whom many believe to be Satoshi, first proposed. The platform would ensure that these applications were secure and not subject to third-party tampering or interference. The platform soon took the name Ethereum, and its first app was the Ether cryptocurrency.

---

2   Vitalik Buterin, "Vitalik Buterin," https://about.me/vitalik_buterin.

Ethereum became a business, as opposed to an idea, at a bitcoin conference held in Miami in early 2014, shortly after the white paper was published. Joe Lubin, at age forty-nine the founding group's oldest member, had a varied business background, including a stint on Wall Street. His business interests also had a creative side. At one point, he was involved with music production in Jamaica.

To probably oversimplify: Vitalik was interested in the technology and its implications. Lubin was the hard-charging, cutthroat semi-suit—although he doesn't wear suits, but branded startup tees—who basically wanted to capitalize on the tech. You might say they needed one another, and their alliance, though short-lived, was highly productive and effective. Lubin's net worth is apparently now in the billions. Vitalik's, though extensive, is considerably less.

I've given a lot of justifiable and necessary emphasis to the alternative or countercultural side of bitcoin. However, it's also critical to realize that, as the original cryptocurrency, bitcoin soon became a magnet for any number of Joe Lubin–type commercialization-focused "suits," including hedge fund managers and institutional investors. These were the people who had money to invest, and bitcoin almost certainly would never have taken off without their participation.

Even if the financial institutions for which these people worked did not condone or directly invest in bitcoin, the people who worked in them did so, ever more regularly. Although most of these bitcoin traders remain anonymous—preserving anonymity is one of the foundational principles of the bitcoin blockchain—some were prominent self-promoters.

Ex-child actor Brock Pierce's story has already been related. Perhaps the best-known investors were the Winklevoss twins, who infused bitcoin with a sizable chunk of the money they won settling the Facebook lawsuit they instituted against Mark Zuckerberg. Their resulting net worth may now be comparable to that of the defendant whom they accused of appropriating the idea behind the world's most successful social network.

SMART CONTRACTS

The technology proposed in Vitalik's white paper had much wider ambitions and implications than those proposed by Satoshi Nakamoto. Vitalik asserts that the principles behind bitcoin were too narrow, and, given what's happened in the crypto and blockchain explosion, it's impossible not to agree with him in principle, if not in every detail.

One way of looking at the underlying concept is that

Ethereum set out to create a worldwide supercomputer. Ethereum is not itself a cryptocurrency, like Ether or Ether Classic, but a platform for creating blockchains. To quote the Ethereum Foundation's website: "Ethereum is a decentralized platform that runs 'smart contracts': applications that run exactly as programmed without any possibility of downtime, censorship, fraud, or third-party interference."

"Smart contract" is a loaded, though frequently used, term. Vitalik has since been quoted as saying that he regrets using it. "Decentralized," on the other hand, is a familiar term basic to the definition of a blockchain. The impossibility of "fraud or third-party interference" means that blocks in a blockchain can't be altered.

What "smart contract" ultimately refers to is code that automates a process that can't be changed. You could debate whether such a process is, or could be, reasonably called a "contract," a word that usually means a legal agreement whose terms, while binding, are frequently altered and often broken. In any event, we're stuck with the term "smart contract," with "smart" apparently meant to imply the technology is fundamentally different from traditional legal contracts.

One way of looking at what happened is that Ethereum reversed bitcoin's chicken and egg. Bitcoin was proposed as a unique use case that was implemented, and that could only be implemented, by the technology that eventually came to be called blockchain. Ethereum was and is a platform for creating decentralized applications, or dApps, applied to any number of different use cases.

It's no surprise that Ethereum's first application was the creation of the Ether cryptocurrency. However, this use case was never meant to be limiting, as bitcoin maximalists insist the bitcoin blockchain was.

The terms of each smart contract Ethereum creates include the technological underpinnings of each blockchain application, which are also called protocols. As previously mentioned, such protocols underlie all the digital communications systems, such as the web, that have become familiar to us through everyday use, although few of us think about the foundational technical layers that support such systems. We simply access a website without ever thinking about TCP/IP (translation: Transmission Control Protocol/Internet Protocol).

DARPA, the Defense Advanced Research Projects Agency, the US Defense Department's research team, was originally responsible for the creation of the internet back in the sixties. The internet was conceived of as a communications network so decentralized that it could not be taken out by a Soviet or other enemy attack. Scientists proposed the underlying protocols and technical standards for the network through a series of so-called RFCs: Requests for Comments. TCP/IP was created by a DARPA RFC. (Like business, the military loves acronyms.)

Similarly, and in conscious imitation, Ethereum set up a system for the proposal, development, and deployment of blockchain protocols and standards, which it calls ERCs: Ethereum Requests for Comments. Each ERC is assigned a number in chronological order: ERC-1, ERC-2, ERC-3, and so on.

ERC-20 was especially important for the development of new cryptocurrency tokens. In my opinion, ERC-20 also has a lot to answer for. The ERC-20 token standard allowed people to develop finite supplies of tokens programmed according to investor preferences. And most investors' primary preference is increasing the value of their tokens.

This approach is called "tokenomics" (token economics). It can be seen as a way of codifying behavioral economic systems—that is, the psychological and sociocultural factors that influence economic decisions—when creating crypto tokens. What this means in practice is that the individuals or organizations that create a cryptocurrency system consisting of non-bitcoin tokens can define or establish the value of a token when it is issued and, to a certain extent, how that value will change over time.

CAVEAT ICO

In the wake of ERC-20, the creation and issuing of new cryptocurrency tokens exploded. Not all these were issued through Ethereum, but even many non-Ethereum tokens were developed on ERC-20 principles. The crypto-financiers who created these tokens recognized the ERC-20 standard could be used to presell tokens for what they claimed to be a utility, or "utility tokens" for short.

What does this mean? Let's return to the analogy of pre-paying for a membership to a golf course that doesn't yet exist. The sellers say they intend to use these pre-payments to build the course. However, it's possible the sellers haven't secured the land or decided on a name for the course when they start preselling memberships. In some cases—more than we'd like to believe—the sellers had no intention of doing so, and the issuance of the token was nothing more or less than a scam.

A common name for this process applied to cryptocurrency is an ICO: initial coin offering. ICOs proliferated beyond belief, especially in 2017. The process became a crazy way for people, for a short time, to cheat the system by raising money through the presales of tokens before the networks, products, or services the buyer was supposedly obtaining a share of were in development. These "utilities"—networks, products, and services—might never see the light of day and in many cases didn't.

The crypto world soon saw the advent of countless ideas, white papers, scams, and consortiums raising hundreds of millions of dollars. The most money was probably raised by Tezos, a crypto blockchain established by Arthur and Kathleen Breitman: a record-breaking $232 million.[3] Tezos was structured as a Swiss foundation that would take in the money invested and fund the Breitmans' private company. The Breitmans are now defendants in some very high-profile class-action lawsuits.

To be clear, many ICOs were quite legitimate and had genuinely intended to use the funds raised to build products and infrastructure. Others had no such goal and were simply fraudulent. They would raise their $5, $50, or $100 million and then claim that they had been hacked—a high-tech version of an exit scam. The website would suddenly shut down, never to reappear, or in some cases, display phallic images with the words, "Got you!"

Crypto is designed not to be traced, and it's therefore often impossible to prove whether there was a hack or not. In some cases, the "founders" liquidated the funds, transferred them to their own wallets or accounts, and disappeared. This is where the concept "sh*tcoin"—a crypto token with no value because its creators had no

---

3   Thijs Maas, "The Curious Tale of Tezos—from a $232 MILLION ICO to 4
     Class Action Lawsuits," *Hacker Noon*, April 6, 2018, https://hackernoon.com/
     the-curious-tale-of-tezos-from-a-232-million-ico-to-4-class-action-lawsuits-6f411b7aad7e.

intention of building a genuine profitable product or network—comes from.

This was all happening very fast, and in America, the SEC was way behind the curve and failed to issue any real guidance. It was only late in 2018, once things were already well underway, that the SEC started filing its first injunctions and cease-and-desist orders against unregistered exchanges. Those smart enough to play it safe knew that these sorts of operations would either need to spend millions in maintaining somewhat undefined and ambiguous regulatory compliance, or would have to be based in other countries more tolerant of financial secrecy or further along in their crypto legislation, such as Malta, Singapore, or Switzerland, where the Breitmans set up shop.

A hilarious satirical video that appeared on LinkedIn shows a fellow sitting in the middle of the desert with a lemonade stand. A thirsty customer comes up and gives him a dollar, asking, "Can I buy a lemonade?" The lemonade vendor responds, "No. To buy a lemonade, you have to get lemoncoins." Discussion ensues, with the would-be buyer asking how he can obtain lemoncoins. An obviously no-goodnik foreigner appears out of nowhere and says, "Oh, you just have to put your ID and social security number on this exchange, and I'll get you some lemoncoins. But it'll take three to five days. We won't send you a notification, so just check back on the exchange in seven days."

The truth hurts. In the early days, the exchanges where you could get your hands on some of these tokens were often more than a little sketchy. You didn't know where half of them were based, and, now that you think about it, they were probably giving away your personal information on a know your customer (KYC) basis. Some governments require verifying the identity of a business's clients or customers, and others don't. For bitcoin maximalists, however, the whole point of bitcoin tokens is privacy, anonymity, resistance to censorship, and not being able to be tracked. A blockchain ID shouldn't have your social security number, driver's license number, date of birth, or photo on it. *Caveat emptor!*

UTILITY AND SECURITY TOKENS

Many of the problems ICOs caused stemmed from an often-intentional blurring of the distinction between "utility tokens" and "security tokens." Even the use of the same term, "token," in both cases led to confusion.

Essentially, ICOs were conflating two important, but fundamentally different ideas often at odds with one another. The incentives of developers of utility-based crypto platforms and speculative investors were not and simply could not be aligned.

A "utility token" is a coin or other marker that has utility, meaning a stable value, on an existing platform. For example, if you are using a token to monitor usage and measure the utility of, for example, an electric grid, the token's value should be relatively stable. It shouldn't be worth one dollar one day and one hundred dollars the next.

Familiar examples of "utility tokens" are airline, hotel chain, and other reward-points systems. The reward points have a relatively stable value within an already-established organization or structure, such as an airline, hotel chain, or at Starbucks. You can't redeem your American Airlines points at Southwest, but you clearly can and do accrue and redeem them when you take American Airlines' flights.

A crypto utility token is similar. It works within a closed-loop ecosystem and has a stable value.

When you buy a security token, on the other hand and as the name implies, you make an investment in an enterprise in hopes of making a profit. There is both an overlap and a distinction between making an investment in a security with the intention of making a profit and pure speculation, which involves trading a financial instrument in a volatile market in the hope or expectation of high returns. (There's more on the distinction between investing and speculating in securities in the next chapter.)

Again, you don't want a utility token to be worth one dollar one day and one hundred dollars the next. But if you are a speculative investor, that's precisely what you want your crypto token to do—gain as much value in as short a time as possible.

When ICOs issued tokens on a preselling basis, purely speculative craziness set in. The network on which presold ICO tokens were supposed to be exchanged was not only not yet in existence but, in many cases, not even under development and never intended to be. The tokens were issued purely so their prices, rather than their real value, would go up.

The US Supreme Court developed the so-called Howey Test to determine whether certain transactions qualify as investment contracts or securities. A crypto "security token" meets the Howey Test definition of a security: an investment in an enterprise made with the expectation of a profit. Although the SEC came a little late to the party, it eventually ruled that crypto security tokens are fundraising vehicles, a means of raising venture, institutional, or real estate investment capital, and therefore must meet SEC regulations.

While ICOs were fundamentally flawed, their demise wasn't the end of new, creative fundraising vehicles. Largely as a workaround to meet SEC requirements, we saw the rise of "security token offerings," which allowed owners of assets like businesses, real estate, or even art to sell securitized tokens as either Reg D or Reg A+ offerings. Such offerings relax certain standards and involve greater risks than, for instance, issuing and buying an S&P 500 stock.

These tokenized securities actually do offer a number of benefits to individuals, companies, and investors. Investors in and founders of startups, as well as early employees awarded stock, must typically wait for a liquidation event, such as an IPO or company sale, to realize liquid value from their holdings. Often this can take up to a decade or more, and many times payday never arrives. Tokenized equity, however, allows for more fluid secondary transactions in such holdings. Tokenized equity can also bring greater fluidity and liquidity to real estate holdings, a historically illiquid market.

Beyond security token offerings, we have seen the emergence of countless other types of token offerings, such as stablecoins, which, to avoid volatility and scamming, are tied to or backed either by a fiat currency, such as the US dollar, or other cryptocurrencies. In September 2018, the Winklevoss twins' company, Gemini Trust, issued an early stablecoin, the Gemini Dollar, which was collateralized with US currency. Other offerings include platform tokens, natural-asset tokens backed by gold or other precious metals, and crypto-fiat currencies.[4]

EVOLUTIONARY SPIN-OFFS

Returning to Ethereum: a separation between Vitalik and Lubin was almost inevitable and didn't take long to occur. The idealistic Vitalik set up Ethereum as a not-for-profit foundation, which he felt was the best vehicle for enabling the platform to genuinely transform the global economy.

Having probably already made several billion dollars in the venture, Lubin split off in 2015 and founded a Brooklyn-based for-profit corporation called Consen-Sys, short for Consensus Systems. Its mission is building Ethereum-based blockchain apps or systems for any number of different industries and verticals. It quickly grew to be one of the largest blockchain companies in the

---

4   Alex Tapscott, "Cryptocurrency Is Just One of Seven Types of Cryptoassets You Should Know," *Quartz*, July 25, 2018, https://qz.com/1335481/cryptocurrency-is-just-one-of-seven-types-of-cryptoassets-you-should-know/. Definitions of many of these terms can be found in this book's online glossary.

world and may have had up to two thousand employees before a significant layoff at the very end of 2018.

ConsenSys-launched companies were often funded through ICOs issuing genuine utility tokens. Lubin may be a businessman first and foremost, but, as his background in the music industry shows, he also has artistic leanings. One of their first ICOs was actually the first crowdfunded film, produced and shot in Italy with an Italian director.

Breaker (previously SingularDTV), another ConsenSys-launched company, focused on digital rights and fractional payments to people in artistic supply chains, such as musicians. The company's products are meant to help every individual who participates in creating an asset to monetize it, countering a trend that has been plaguing many artists such as musicians since the advent of digital and especially streaming technology.

While Ethereum is the underlying not-for-profit blockchain platform, ConsenSys is a for-profit blockchain conglomerate focusing—if that's the word—everywhere at once, in both the consumer (B2C) and enterprise (B2B) businesses. In the enterprise space, although most of its revenue has come from professional services, it has also launched supply chain, legal, and financial blockchain "dApps."

Another of Ethereum's founders, Gavin Wood, a British programmer who was its first CTO, has also gone his own way. In 2015, he and Jutta Steiner founded Parity Technologies, whose stated mission is building a blockchain-enabled Web 3.0 not subject to the monopolistic tendencies of current major players such as Google and Facebook.

Wood has called the technology underlying this initiative "Polkadot." Not to dive too deeply, the Polkadot "lightpaper" proposes the creation of so-called parachains, which are chains or systems of semi-independent blockchains. The thesis is that there will be many mini-blockchains, all based on the Ethereum platform or virtual machine.

Parity's mission is to make blockchain systems far more usable by promoting large-scale interoperability among different blockchains. Parity has also released "Substrate," a framework to supply developers with the latest blockchain-building technologies.

ERC-721 AND OTHER BLOCKCHAIN PROTOCOLS

The other most significant ERC in the Ethereum system, after ERC-20, is ERC-721, which is the protocol or standard for issuing unique, non-fungible tokens. This is the protocol that led to the creation of digital collectibles such as CryptoKitties, whose relative uniqueness and scarcity, as is the case with many collectibles, has increased their value.

ERC-721 brings us back to some of crypto's origins in gaming, which involved exchanges such as Reddit boards, where in-game assets could be traded, bought, and sold. As discussed earlier, forming such "communities of practice" seems a fundamental human impulse, one upon which eBay's niche communities—one of the platform's biggest strengths—were built.

Vitalik Buterin himself was a *World of Warcraft* player prior to founding Ethereum. The almost quaint and hippie-ish sensibility associated with Pokémon cards and some gaming communities seems to have affected Ethereum and its adherents: purple T-shirts, rainbow-hued logos, unicorns, and the like. This sensibility may have found its fullest expression in crypto-collectibles.

THE KILLER USE CASE

Just to be clear: not all the newer cryptocurrencies are based on Ethereum's ERC-20 protocol. Some were created for different aims and purposes. Monero and Zcash are focused on privacy and anonymity, which have now, some say, been eroded in bitcoin. A core group of bitcoin developers later developed Decred, a new cryptocurrency meant to stay true to certain core values of the Satoshi white paper, while allowing some innovations in areas such as governance.

On the cultural side, a joke I always make is that the killer use case for ERC-20 tokens and ICOs was the crypto conference. I've been running a company in the crypto-blockchain space for quite some time and remember when there were just four or so relevant conferences a year. You could count them on the fingers of one hand.

Once 2017 came around, there was a conference every day. There might even be five a day in a given city. Meet-ups and education events sprang up left and right. While this kept me very busy as a speaker, it seemed the conferences themselves, or their organizers, had the upper hand. They were charging both presenters and attendees exorbitant registration fees, because everyone was trying to get their coin in front of people and pitch it onstage.

That's died down now. While these conferences and meetups are not going to go away entirely, the boom—all the ICOs and white papers—is definitely over. And I predict that as the quantity goes down, the quality will go up.

As a speaker, and in writing this book, my interest is not only in talking about and exploring the technology. The reason I'm excited about blockchain in the first place is that it both represents and is bringing about a much bigger global paradigmatic social shift from centralization to decentralization. It's not just a matter of supply and demand, which is the way investors were looking at crypto ICOs, but how these trends are going to change our culture and people's behavior.

In this respect, the significance of the ERC-20 protocol and ICOs very much has to do, once again, with the thesis of the Union Square Ventures white paper (what else?) entitled "The Myth of the Infrastructure Phase." To quote authors Dan Grant and Nick Grossman's succinct summary: "First, apps inspire new infrastructure. Then infrastructure enables new apps."

Web 3.0, the crypto and blockchain web, is not "just" in the infrastructure phase. As I see it, the ICOs that grew out of the ERC-20 protocol, as irresponsible as some were, were also applications that have inspired the further development of the Web 3.0 infrastructure. That infrastructure will, in turn, enable new and better apps that will affect the way we communicate and transact business. Crazes and trends like the ICOs, whatever their weaknesses and faults, almost inevitably lead to an infrastructure build-out.

Many past and current crypto apps are relatively trivial. A digital wallet that facilitates paying for a cup of coffee is no big deal. If Union Square Ventures and other big venture capital groups made major investments in CryptoKitties, they weren't investing in the CryptoKitties themselves, but in what they stood for.

There have been absurdities as well as scams along the way, as when the Long Island Iced Tea Company changed its name to the Long Blockchain Company. In a sense, this seems like nothing more than a joke. What does blockchain have to do with a sugary drink? In another sense, it isn't, because, ridiculous as the name change was, it marked a significant cultural shift—as well as an uptick in the value of the company stock.

Investors ask me all the time, "Sam, what are the picks and shovels of the blockchain industry? That's what I want to invest in." They're referring to the California Gold Rush, where those who supplied the mining infrastructure—notably Levi Strauss with his denim pants—generally made much more money than the prospectors themselves.

However, in 1849, people had already been mining and prospecting for gold for millennia. Building a transformative technology is more of a chicken-and-egg or app-and-infrastructure scenario. One thing I am confident of is that as Web 3.0 evolves, different kinds of blockchains will develop. That process is already well underway.

Both bitcoin and Ethereum are public and open blockchains. Permissioned blockchains directed at certain industries and verticals are at an even earlier stage of development. They will become increasingly important and, in my opinion, can do so without violating the "decentralized autonomous" principles upon which any genuine blockchain is built. Actually, I sometimes wonder if I really believe this myself, but I do know permissioned blockchains are a way forward that deserves further exploration.

In the short history of crypto to date, there have been ups and downs, scams and opportunities. There have also been plenty of crypto and blockchain critics. Let's hear what they have to say, since anyone really interested in this new technology needs to pay attention to and seriously evaluate their opinions.

CHAPTER 9

NO-COINERS AND CRYPTO-SKEPTICS

Thomas Edison is revered as "the father of invention." Having filed over a thousand patents in his lifetime, the title is richly deserved. But he wasn't always venerated.

When Edison enhanced existing designs and first proposed the commercial application of the electric light bulb, a British Parliamentary committee dismissed the invention as "unworthy of practical or scientific attention." Others called him a shill and a sham. However, with continued development of the electrical-grid infrastructure and standardization of the Edison screw, the interface connecting the light bulb to the lighting system, the public began adopting a technology that is ubiquitous today.

The blockchain space is in an iterative cycle of the development and standardization of its protocols, infrastructure, and commercial applications, similar to the seventy years of innovations and tweaks involving hundreds of inventors that ultimately brought us the light bulb.

To put it simply, many of us still think of blockchain like Edison's naysayers thought of the light bulb: something that burns out quickly, works only with custom-made lamps, and has to be powered by dedicated generators.

Unsurprisingly, this early in the cycle, haters want to hate. Meet the "no-coiners."

"No-coiners" come in two overlapping varieties: those who don't own cryptocurrency and aren't interested in doing so, and those who think crypto is little or nothing more than a hoax and a scam. A lot of journalists are no-coiners of the first variety because they want to keep an unbiased perspective. Perhaps the most prominent member of the second variety is Warren Buffett, America's most esteemed investor and investment advisor.

POINT–COUNTERPOINT

In his opposition to crypto, it's possible Warren Buffett could be giving great investment advice and that most everyone who gets involved in crypto is just getting duped. In the last chapter, we saw that ICOs involved a fair amount of scamming. However, the situation, in my opinion, is not so cut-and-dried.

What I understand about Warren Buffett from reading about and watching documentaries on him is that he may be the most astute student of financial trends in our time. He has a historical bias: what can we learn about the ways markets have operated in the recent and not-so-recent past?

Cryptocurrency, however, has a very short history. Historical data, which the finance industry relies on when doing analysis, is still fairly sparse in the blockchain and cryptocurrency markets.

It makes sense that someone like Warren Buffett would consider an asset or vehicle like crypto, where there isn't much historical precedent or data on market trends, to be an incredibly risky investment. Bitcoin, the original cryptocurrency, was first issued in 2009, but didn't really start taking off until 2013. Everybody, including mainstream media and Uber drivers, got interested when prices went through the roof in 2017, but a lot of what crypto white papers and thought leaders have to say on the subject is and can't be anything other than speculative.

As we've seen, "speculative" is a word with a number of meanings. A May 2018 CNBC article quotes Buffett as saying, "If you buy something like Bitcoin or cryptocurrency you don't have anything that is producing anything, you're just hoping the next guy pays more. You aren't investing when you do that, you're speculating."[1]

Buffett may have become such a trusted investment advisor in part because he draws a strong line between investment and speculation. However, "investors" of all kinds, including professional investors, seem to have nothing against making money through financial speculation. The whole day trading industry is built on it.

Buffett's comment was made in May 2018, during, although at the tail end of, the bitcoin bubble. A lot of people were mesmerized by bitcoin's rise. Many invested in bitcoin and other crypto hoping to triple their holdings in short order. It was a classic "get rich quick" scheme.

What was and continues to go on in crypto looks very much like traditional trading-room floors. It might be objected that when speculators trade commodities, they are trading something "real": an actual shipment of oil or soybeans.

It could also be argued that non-fungible tokens, crypto-

---

1   Ali Montag, "Warren Buffett explains one thing people still don't understand about bitcoin," CNBC, May 1, 2018, https://www.cnbc.com/2018/05/01/warren-buffett-bitcoin-isnt-an-investment.html.

collectibles, and cryptocurrency in general have no real relationship to physical assets. However, asset-backed tokens representing gold or oil, or security tokens that represent ownership in real estate do, in fact, symbolize physical value. It could also be argued that the difference between speculating in commodities and crypto is not that great, especially in a financial and socioeconomic environment that digital technology has completely transformed.

There are hybrid "proof-of-work/proof-of-stake" crypto products such as Decred—"decentralized credit"—where a financial stake also gives you the right to vote on fundamental issues, such as whether the currency should be forked or not. It's almost as if Decred stakeholders held stock in a conventional corporation. There are, of course, differences: votes take place via stakeholder computers chosen at random. There are also similarities: if your computer participates in a vote, you get paid a "staking" award, which is not, but in some respects feels a lot like, interest. There are now countless "staking as a service" firms that use various mechanisms to stake coins across networks and earn rewards.

SHIFTING DEFINITIONS

Of course, either/or definitions, like conventional stock versus crypto stakeholding, have limited applicability when paradigms are shifting, as they are now. To tell the truth, following my initial foray through gaming, I was a no-coiner myself for a very long time. I was so focused on building infrastructure and products that I didn't get involved in trading-cycle hype.

My entry point, like that of most early adopters, was buying bitcoin. The thing is—and I feel this is an important distinction—I didn't see this as speculation. When I bought bitcoin the first time, early on, I was doing research, just as I did research on other, somewhat related digital realms, such as Second Life or the dark web.

If you spend five cents to buy something online, you're not thinking of stashing it away because one day, like the first bitcoin Pizza, it's going to be worth hundreds of millions of dollars. My approach wasn't that of a speculator, gambler, or investor. I was buying bitcoin, but I might just as well have been acquiring Second Life Linden dollars, bought on an exchange so I could buy a ticket to go to an in-world Fatboy Slim concert.

I was thinking very much in terms of utility, and in this I'm far from alone in the crypto community, certainly among early adopters. I didn't buy thinking or hoping the price would go up. I assumed the currency was stable enough or, rather, that it had a stable value in its digital sphere or "world" at that time, which would enable me to do what

I wanted to do. I was investing rather than speculating, in Warren Buffett's sense, and continue to invest when acquiring Decred and similar cryptocurrencies.

We now have "stablecoins" and other crypto whose value is pegged to fiat currencies such as the US dollar: one token equals one dollar. A variety of economic mechanisms helps assure this price stability. The goal of many bitcoin fundamentalists is for bitcoin itself to be a "stable coin." People would transact micropayments in the denomination of a "Satoshi" or the lowest bitcoin unit, which, as we've seen, equals one hundred millionth of a single bitcoin (0.00000001 BTC). Unlike fiat currencies, such as the US dollar, whose lowest denomination is a cent, cryptocurrencies are far more flexible in their denominations and can therefore unlock value and new business models based on micropayments.

Not all no-coiners are skeptics. My brother was one of the first people I knew who got into bitcoin, because he was a gamer like me and also mined the currency. His computer provided "proof of work." Then he sold his bitcoin at some point and didn't buy it again. Technically, he's a no-coiner at the moment, but that doesn't mean he was never involved.

Then there's my businessman father. He'd never buy bitcoin, but I did convince him to invest in a "mining" company that's part of the bitcoin infrastructure. He's still skeptical, however, and loves sending me sensationalist mainstream media articles with headlines like "Crypto Is Dead!"

DUE DILIGENCE AND BLACK HATS

Nouriel Roubini, the professor at NYU's Stern School of Business we've encountered before, is, along with Warren Buffett, the other most prominent "no-coiner" crypto critic. He just hates the stuff with little of the equanimity that the more revered Buffett, for all his criticism, displays when talking about its risks.

Roubini is a self-proclaimed expert who has testified against crypto in Congress. He believes that large token holders, or "whales," are manipulating the entire crypto market, including, but not limited to, bitcoin. They can do so, he contends, because the caps on these markets are so small. In Roubini's opinion, "whales" basically pump crypto markets, reap the benefits, and then dump their holdings. Everyone else in the market is at their mercy and left holding the bag. From his perspective, crypto markets are fully centralized and nothing more than scams.

As we saw in the last chapter, ICO and other crypto scams have undoubtedly taken place. These shouldn't be swept under the rug, because we need to learn from our mistakes. However, some no-coiners think cryptocurrency itself is a sham. Many feel the same way about blockchain: that it is nothing more than a glorified database. A third group deprecates crypto, but sees value in its underlying blockchain or distributed-ledger technology.

In my opinion, such black-and-white negative stances betray fundamental ignorance. The counter-argument is to point out the similarities between crypto and the traditional system of financial markets. There have been booms and busts ever since before the emergence of stock exchanges. In boom times, people go a little crazy and, proverbially, fools and their money are soon parted.

Due diligence applies as much to crypto as to traditional investments, yet many investors, even professional ones, don't do proper or even adequate vetting and research. That's dangerous in the digital age, when it is easier to fake "facts" than ever before.

Black-hat marketers, with a five-hundred-strong team in Bangladesh, say, can literally create fake people with fake histories. I'm serious about this because I've seen it firsthand. LinkedIn accounts and other social media histories are faked, as are blog posts, so it appears these are people with a real history at companies like IBM and universities like Stanford. The marketers then create entire fake businesses to raise money from unsophisticated investors. Sometimes, they make it appear that there are more companies operating in a given market than there really are. It becomes very hard to tell whether there is an actual person or company behind a digital identity that has been so comprehensively developed.

A company called TruStory has been launched to investigate and validate these sorts of claims. Its original mission was to help investors do their due diligence on ICOs, but they have expanded to validating any claims made on the internet. For instance, if I want to claim that I made it to the summit of Mount Everest, I could easily Photoshop an image of myself hanging out with prayer flags at the peak, which TruStory could then debunk.

TruStory is a potentially valuable service at a time when "fake news," and especially the "deep fakes" just described, are proliferating. I recently met with a prominent investor who showed me some interesting demos from a company in his portfolio. The technology is intended to help newscasters translate broadcasts and studios dub movies in real time, without mismatching what is being said with mouth and facial movements. The technology processes the vocal and data feed, translates what is being said, say from Spanish into English, and then both translates the dialogue and changes the broadcaster's or actor's mouth movements, all in real time.

If you think about the potential misuse of this technology, you might conclude that we're one minute to midnight on the doomsday clock of online trust. Black-hat marketers could create enough fake identities to fill up a small city, Photoshopping life accomplishments. Instagram influencers could pay a hundred dollars an hour to sit in a private jet parked on a runway pretending they're actually flying. A video broadcast could be altered in real time to change a newscaster's content. More ominously, the broadcast of a leader of one government in conflict with another could be hacked so that his statements are made to appear to be a declaration of war.

The point is that due diligence and trust are always of the utmost importance. However, it is becoming increasingly difficult to do due diligence with the assumption that you are actually getting to the facts on the ground.

It's all too easy to see how this approach might be used to validate the existence of a real team behind a scam ICO. During the ICO boom, there really wasn't much in place to facilitate due diligence. Know your customer (KYC) requirements then started being instituted and would-be investors had to be validated as having real identities. For many, such vetting techniques came too late.

I know firsthand that a screenshot image of myself showed up on a few fake ICO scam websites, saying I was a company advisor, which I was not. This was all too common during the ICO rush, and I'm far from the only one who was subjected to reputation or identity harvesting.

Even in this frightening new world, however, investment due diligence still comes down to basics. If, upon reflection and a little research, you can say, "I don't know, I've never heard of these people; I've never met them or seen them," then I'd look into it more deeply.

Have there been ICOs that scammed their investors? Certainly. Could digital technology be used to scam people in the future? Of course. Any new technology or idea can be misused to burn people. This happened frequently when new technologies were introduced in the past.

Does that mean all cryptocurrency is a scam? That's quite a strong and equally inaccurate statement. In fact, crypto and blockchain purport to be building a trust economy in a world where trust is in short supply. Let's face it, we can't trust anything anymore: not what we read in the news and not what we buy from the grocery store.

BUBBLES AND BUSTS

Let's also take a historical perspective, just like Warren Buffett. Were there stock market bubbles that burst in 2008, 2001, and several other occasions, notably 1929?

Certainly, which is to say that there are just as many similarities as differences between the ups and downs of traditional exchanges and crypto bull runs and bear markets.

No-coiners like Nouriel Roubini say, "Cryptocurrency is carefully orchestrated to create a bubble, take advantage of everyone, and steal money." That's their perspective: the global scam.

However, it's hard to call what happened with bitcoin in 2017 a bubble. Bitcoin has had both bull and long bear markets. To take a historical perspective again: those who put substantial money into bitcoin in the early days saw it go from a fraction of a penny to a dollar and made significant gains. In 2017, we saw bitcoin go from $6,000 to $20,000, but something like this had already happened three times before.

Bitcoin is actually on a relatively consistent upward trend. The speculators, who want continually higher valuations, react to downturns by saying, "Oh my god, this is terrible. The whole market is doomed."

People who have been involved in bitcoin for a while believe that it will continue to trend upward in the long run. The actual goal, depending on who you ask, is the creation of a stable global currency or store of value that institutional investors and others trust and rely on to the extent that they're willing to build other financial products with it. It's meant to be a global currency that transcends national and corporate bounds and restrictions.

Creating a new system of such scope is a massive undertaking, something bitcoin has already accomplished. Bitcoin has shown there's a genuine alternative to fiat currency. Then comes the backlash: cryptocurrency is somehow no good as a financial instrument, as a technology, or both. In fact, bitcoin has been in production for ten years and is still going strong. It's relatively solid.

BLACK MARKETS AND ILLEGAL TRADE

What no-coiners' problem actually is, in my opinion, is fear of change. Perhaps they have so much tied up with the current system that they believe it's incredibly risky to innovate. The truth is that innovation *is* risky. It's also inevitable.

Let's look at the risky or dark side first. No-coiners persist in making an argument that goes all the way back to the early days: bitcoin is only for criminals and drug dealers.

Satoshi Nakamoto's white paper proposes a technology for decentralizing financial transactions. It came out almost strategically in response to the 2008 financial crisis. The timing and marketing of bitcoin were near perfect, whether planned or not.

What the white paper proposed was not something meant to support criminals. It was a statement that the current financial system couldn't really be trusted due to its centralized points of failure.

There's no doubt decentralization may help hide criminal activity. However, its greater purpose is to protect against both the failure and abuse of centralized institutional power. It's simply not true, if you're cautious about government power, that you're by definition trying to do something illegal. Decentralization is also a means of checking the power of large, centralized corporations, including massive internet companies, which are probably in violation of antitrust laws that now appear increasingly difficult to enforce.

Look at the control that companies like Facebook and Google exert over our access to information. Small- and medium-sized retailers are now practically obligated to list and sell their products through Amazon. If Amazon then sees your product is doing extraordinarily well, they're in a position to produce it themselves and undercut you.

However, there's no doubt drug dealers and other

criminals did use bitcoin in its early days to conduct transactions on the dark web through encrypted, underground networks such as the Silk Road, which Ross Ulbricht developed beginning in 2010. Five years later, he was charged and then convicted of drug trafficking, money laundering, and even conspiracy to commit murder, although that last conviction has recently been overturned. I went on the Silk Road to do research, and it definitely felt dark and scary.

However, black markets have predated bitcoin by millennia. Illegal trade is one of the biggest global economies and has apparently been around since the dawn of man. To claim that bitcoin somehow created illicit black-market trade is absurd. It may have made illegal trade easier to transact for a time, but if something else came along to make such trafficking still more efficient, bitcoin would be dropped in a second. The illegal activity, which cannot be condoned, in a way proves that bitcoin was, at least at the time, a really effective way of making transactions without someone looking over your shoulder.

That being said, if I were a criminal, I wouldn't use bitcoin at all. I'd stick to good old cash. The fact that every bitcoin transaction is unalterable and a matter of public record makes criminal transaction somewhat risky, in my opinion, even if your wallet address doesn't reveal your identity.

I've written extensively about markets in illicit trade. I interviewed former US State Department officials and worked with the UN. When I co-founded Chronicled, one of our first tasks was to combat counterfeit goods and then to focus on bringing trust to pharma and other global supply chains.

Counterfeit goods—luxury goods, pharmaceuticals, cigarettes, art, car parts, you name it—are markets worth nearly half a trillion a year. This existed long before bitcoin was created and contributes to geopolitical instability all around the world.

When you buy that cheap, fake iPhone charger on Amazon, do you think you might be fueling a war? When you wear glittery eye shadow or drive a car with speckled paint, do you think about how the mica in that glitter was mined by a nine-year-old child in a rural province of India?

When you eat almost any processed food, do you think about the palm oil it contains, which has likely contributed to the destruction of Malaysian rain forests and other large-scale deforestation? When someone in a country with a marginal healthcare infrastructure buys much-needed medication from someone on the street, and that drug turns out to be counterfeit, do we stop to consider the harm being caused? When you eat fresh-caught salmon, do you think about how fishing is an industry involved with human trafficking and indentured servitude? After all, you can't go anywhere if you're trapped on a boat in the middle of international waters, can you?

I think you get the picture.

I'm not sharing these examples to be a Debbie Downer, but to demonstrate how much of the illicit trade that we see today was neither created nor enabled by cryptocurrency or other alternative currency markets. It was enabled in large part by the trust gaps our vast global supply chains and current economic system create.

When we made the switch from localized trade—where we could see what was being made and knew who was making it—to an industrialized globalized world—where products are manufactured on assembly lines, often with atrocious working conditions—trust gaps were inevitably created.

Take a few steps back and understand that we now operate in an environment where we have vast and complex global networks, where brands often don't know their suppliers or suppliers' suppliers, and illicit trade has proliferated. Frankly, blockchain technology has done more to combat illicit trade than it has to enable it.

If a binary, black-and-white perspective is taken, then,

yes, bitcoin has helped facilitate illegal trade. However, like technology, legal and belief systems can change quickly and even suddenly, as seen in marijuana legalization in Canada and many US states.

CHANGE AND FEAR OF CHANGE

The fundamental change in the blockchain technology behind crypto facilitates is decentralization. Today's world is both globalized and centralized. We rely on centralized institutions for everything from our finances to the food that we eat and the information we access. We rely on centralized institutions, but do we trust them? The frightening reality is that we trust them less and less. People don't like to think about it, but that's the current reality. Facebook hacks, food recalls, election fraud: all this is creating a come-to-Jesus moment. Some things just aren't working, and we might as well admit it.

Then again, decentralization is also frightening. It feels libertarian in some ways and socialistic in others, and that scares people on many different sides of the political spectrum. Decentralization is a bit Robin Hood–esque, and all we can do is hope that Robin Hood really is the good guy and not the Sheriff of Nottingham in disguise.

Confusion and contradiction are inevitable during times of major transformation. On the one hand, some folks raise a rallying cry of "let's take down the powers that be and the intermediaries who are making all the money." But when you look at those eager to get on board, they include large corporations that basically want to optimize their current, quite profitable systems.

While this is confusing, it's all taking place in a larger context, and we all, including no-coiners, need to expand our perspective. The narrow perspective—which has validity in its own context—focuses on scam ICOs and people being taken for a ride. The wider perspective looks at the processes by which innovations and paradigm shifts occur.

The concept of mass production was around before Henry Ford, in the meat-packing industry, for example. Ford applied it to car manufacturing and, within twenty years, the time it took to build an automobile was reduced from nine hours to twelve minutes. Within that twenty years, any car manufacturer that didn't adopt Ford's system went out of business.

The point isn't to use scare tactics and say, "If you're a no-coiner, you're going to end up left in the dust the same way Ford left his competitors." However, there are many times in history where a technology manifests out of an idea and then totally revolutionizes how things are both done and thought about.

Current assumptions are deeply ingrained, nevertheless. Ford's innovation led to global supply chains with big, centralized manufacturers and teams of people on production lines that are modularized every step of the way. This is what we've grown up with, and the tendency is to believe that "these are the facts on the ground." This is what we perceive our reality to be. People also used to believe the world was flat. The way things are done now has not always been and will not always be the case.

To take a small, but telling case: look at New York City cab companies and their monopoly on taxi medallions. Things were working great, in the sense that they were clearly making money. Then Uber came and along with the idea of putting an underutilized asset—cars parked on streets or sitting in garages—to work.

This happens time and time again. The people who innovate are able to see past the constraints and limitations of current belief systems.

Crypto and blockchain are quite new and volatile. They're grounded in a completely digital realm, which is not what most people think of as "reality." This makes them difficult for most people to grasp.

I'm not suggesting that Warren Buffett himself is necessarily having trouble grasping "digital reality." Stocks are digitized. The money in my bank account is just zeros and ones. If I ask for my balance, the ATM shows me how much is in the account, but that money is not really there, only "kind of" there.

However, as a species, human beings are physical and tactile beings, and this may be one root of the issues no-coiners have with crypto. Bitcoin is not a physical currency. It doesn't have a physical embodiment like a dollar bill, or tea brick, or shell. The absence of physicality can make crypto hard to trust.

Cryptocurrencies are algorithms running on computers in server farms. This is difficult to grasp in both senses of the word: hard to understand and impossible to put your arms around. When you invest in a stock, you make the assumption you're investing in a real company making real things. However, crypto remains part of a much larger socio-technological shift that's happening as surely as the sun rises in the east, however hard that shift may be on occasion to think about and understand.

When transformative paradigm shifts occur, they're always hard to grasp. The term "paradigm shift" was introduced in 1962 by Thomas Kuhn, a historian of science, in his book *The Structure of Scientific Revolutions*. Kuhn defined a paradigm shift as a fundamental change in the basic concepts of a scientific discipline. Examples are the Copernican insight that the earth revolves around the sun rather than vice versa and the introduction of quantum physics in the early twentieth century.

The term "paradigm shift" itself recursively created a paradigm shift in the way scientists looked at science. (Incidentally, as basic as the concept of "science" is to the way we now perceive reality, the term "scientist" didn't come into use until 1833.) For the most part, scientists are at least now prepared to conceive that their basic principles—the way they look at reality—are bound to change at some point. Why should our financial and political systems be any different, especially at a time of fundamental technological transformation?

However, change is disorienting, and it sometimes seems that the best way to reorient ourselves around the old reality is to use words like "scam" to describe the change that's underway. The word "scam" itself only appeared in the last century—it was added to the Oxford English Dictionary in the 1960s—and has no apparent etymology. There is speculation about the word's origin, but I find it telling that its origin and usage are so recent. Perhaps its introduction coincides with the acceleration of technology. Who knows: this might be a good subject for a doctoral dissertation.

Of course, no-coiners are entitled to their beliefs. You can love crypto or hate crypto. I'm personally intrigued by it and feel it points to a basic new way of thinking about financial and other networked transactions. To think about the financial system in a fundamentally new way doesn't mean you're scamming people.

Bitcoin may or may not survive. It may or may not work in the long run. At the very least, Satoshi Nakamoto's white paper proposed a genuinely new idea that is forcing us to acknowledge that we hold certain beliefs—about the financial system and organizational structures in general—that many of us don't want to acknowledge to be beliefs rather than "reality."

It feels incredibly risky to change proven or existing organizational or corporate structures. The blockchain company I co-founded, Chronicled, is surprisingly traditional. Its home office is in San Francisco, and there is a feeling that that's where everybody needs to be located. I personally feel, however, that the future of work is distributed and decided to move back to the East Coast, where I'm from, and where my personal and professional networks are located. I prefer to work remotely and have helped grow distributed teams numbering in the hundreds. I believe distributed teams and decentralized organizations are the wave of the future, and that companies that aren't dispersed are going to miss out on opportunities to attract talent and cut costs.

There are countless companies and teams in the block-chain space, and they're largely distributed with global teams. Whether they actually have flat hierarchies or not, as some of them claim, is open to debate, but much of what they have done is both innovative and admirable. They've not only shipped code, but also innovated organizational structure, corporate governance, and decision-making processes and tools.

The following may sound a bit ageist, which is a risk I'm willing to take, because I'm also going to be ageist about myself. I feel that the paradigm shifts I've been talking about are most likely to be understood, adopted, and implemented by Gen Z, kids now in high school or younger.

I'm a millennial. Internet adoption started taking off when I was in middle school. There have obviously already been accelerating transitions in my lifetime. Gen Z, however, has grown up completely connected and digitally native. They're the smartphone and *Fortnite*-playing generation. They're also very involved in cryptocurrency and use it intuitively. Some no-coiners of earlier generations see crypto as just a volatile—meaning "bad"—investment vehicle. Gen Z has, and will have, a different perspective. They distrust institutions and demand new models that provide transparency.

INSTITUTIONAL INVESTORS AND REGULATION

The term "investment vehicle" brings us back from speculating about transformation and the future to the topic of financial speculation. Another early, adamant no-coiner was Jamie Dimon, the CEO of JP Morgan. Then he turned on a dime, so to speak, and JP Morgan started investing heavily in bitcoin. They produced an enterprise fork of Ethereum, called Quorum, that many enterprise-grade blockchain companies use as infrastructure. They've also since released their own coin.

Institutional investors are still learning how to deal with, treat, and think about crypto. You can't create the same institutional products or derivatives with it that you can with fiat currency. There's a lot of room for innovation and also a lot to be learned from both an investment and regulatory perspective.

With respect to no-coiners, again, there was very little due diligence at the start of the ICO bubble. Some quite seasoned institutional investors came to me, as a consultant, to vet ICO teams. Some of the scammers would use photos and names of real people—even myself on occasion, as I've mentioned. They would say they were on the advisory board or the team, creating fake LinkedIn profiles and so on.

Institutional investors, the big banks, the hedge

funds—the people who want to make and sell financial products—depend on market regulations. They can't take your 401(k) funds and invest them in markets that aren't regulated. The SEC needs to be on board.

The SEC has been sending out cease and desist letters to almost every ICO exchange launched during 2017. Perhaps the thought here was "better late than never." Fines have been levied, but many of them have been slaps on the wrist: a $75,000 fine for an ICO that may have made hundreds of millions.

The SEC recently announced they're opening an entire resource center for people who are considering doing ICOs or making similar offerings. The hope is that this could be the beginning of an open dialogue between members of the crypto community and Congress, as well as the SEC. The SEC probably realizes it didn't provide much guidance early on.

There are bound to be ongoing tensions between crypto and regulators, and we can only hope that some of that tension will be creative. Blockchain, crypto's backbone, is a technology meant to bypass government and other centralized oversight and regulation. Bitcoin fundamentalists believe that crypto should transcend the government bounds, which, in turn, fuels no-coiner fear and fury.

Again, this is part of a larger movement. A nation-state's boundaries don't really matter, for instance, to multinational corporations—except when they do. The internet was also meant to be a communications medium transcending national boundaries, but it is inevitably affected by national governments and their laws. Just look at Chinese regulation of the web. The movement to transcend national boundaries and regulations yields both scams and innovation.

Many governments started from a position of fear and a no-coiner mentality about crypto. Now we seem to be entering a period when governments are not so quick to take no-coiner positions. If politics is the art of the possible, governments and regulators need and are beginning to acknowledge that cryptocurrency is a reality that needs to be considered and dealt with more reasonably and carefully than in the past.

This is an international issue, of course, not limited to the United States. South Korea banned cryptocurrency and then rescinded its ban. Countries like Switzerland, Singapore, and Malta created favorable legislation and have become crypto havens. Even in the US, states like Wyoming, New Hampshire, and Delaware are moving in this direction: offering guidance and even state-level legislation on crypto-token requirements. A badly needed and genuine dialogue has begun.

PART III

BLOCKCHAIN: THE LINKS ARE SPREADING!

{ CHAPTER 10 }

PARTY LIKE IT'S 1994!

I still remember sitting in the back of my mom's car as a kid, as she called home from her "car phone," thinking, gosh, what a luxury! The idea that she needed a phone in the car so she could chat with her friends or call my grandma while running a five-minute errand seemed ridiculous to my six-year-old self.

Fast-forward through my childhood. That car phone became a mobile phone, which later became a smartphone-sized supercomputer with more computing power than the mainframes used to land men on the moon. And 3G becomes 4G, which becomes 5G. Everything gets faster, smaller, and more powerful, as Moore's law predicted. Not just technology, but communications are evolving right before our eyes.

My parents wouldn't let me have a cell phone in high school, even when I was selected to study at Oxford University as a sixteen-year-old. I arrived in the UK on my own and used a calling card and pay phone to let my parents know I was safe—three days after my actual arrival, much to their dismay. I traveled to France, using internet cafes and word of mouth. Times were simpler then.

While a lot has changed in the last twenty-five years, I believe we're in a unique moment right now, and what's happening is only the beginning.

Blockchain is the backbone of cryptocurrency and is also being developed, in the broader sense, as the backbone of what's being called Web 3.0. Web 3.0 has a catchy ring to it, but what does it mean?

WEB 1.0, 2.0, AND 3.0

The history of the internet and web in all its versions is a history of networking. The early web, Web 1.0, was a network that enabled users to make point-to-point, one-to-one, and peer-to-peer exchanges.

In the good old days, if you wanted to share a photo with someone, you'd send it to them physically, through the US mail. Web 1.0 brought us email. After taking a digital photo, you'd share it with someone by sending an email, to which you attached the file. If you wanted to send a Christmas card, you'd have to send it in an email to multiple recipients or in several emails to each of the people you wanted to be in touch with. The process involved multiple point-to-point connections.

What changed with Web 2.0 was the social network. The rise of Web 2.0 social networks coincided with other technological advances at the time, including cloud servers and mobile phones, which essentially put the internet into everyone's hands any time, any place. Instead of going through the more laborious process of sending a digital photo to individual recipients, point-to-point, you could share it simultaneously with thousands of "friends." The ability to leverage the network effect in this way revolutionized web-based communications.

Blockchain-enabled Web 3.0 is still very much in the early stages of construction. Many thought leaders in the space assert that blockchain brings trust to networking. In my opinion, it's more helpful to look at blockchain not as a technology that enables trust, but one that makes trust unnecessary. The major shift is that you no longer need to trust. You could say blockchain enables "trustless" networks.

We've become accustomed to, and even dependent on, all the conveniences that Web 2.0 social networking has brought us. We've come to take for granted single sign-on, seamless, and often elegant user experiences, and everything moving very quickly.

However, we've also come to realize that all this convenience comes at a price and that a critical part of that price is our privacy. Services like Google and Facebook appear free, but we're paying for them with our data: with information about ourselves, what we do, and how we act. We are the product. What these services do with that data is in their control, not ours.

These companies, along with a few others like Amazon, have essentially become huge data monopolies. This is probably illegal, but it's hard to go after these companies with antitrust laws for a number of reasons, including shifts in the political climate and, perhaps even more significantly, the pre-digital or analog nature of most antitrust legislation.

Google started with search algorithms, returning results that were more useful than those delivered by previous, more primitive search engines. However, its page-rank algorithm also allowed the company to give preferential treatment to certain results. The data from each search is also collected and can be analyzed and applied in any number of ways. Then the company came out with the Chrome browser and the Android mobile operating system, both of which enabled it to track user data more comprehensively, even when you aren't on the search engine.

Facebook also collects massive amounts of data, not only on individuals, but their "friends." All this data enables the company to make recommendations that are often useful and generally lucrative. However, such data can also be used subversively, and the company has come under investigation for not only enabling, but in some cases possibly colluding in voter manipulation during the 2016 presidential election. All this is quite unnerving.

Amazon's ability to undercut competition in any consumer product has already been mentioned. It's damned if you do and damned if you don't. If you're selling a product, you've got to be on Amazon. If the data Amazon collects on your sales proves the product worthwhile, the company can then essentially take over your market with its own competitive offering.

PEER-TO-PEER: TRUST NOT REQUIRED

Web 2.0 forces users to trust these companies with their data, whether they like it or not. Blockchain-based Web 3.0 is being built to eliminate the need for such trust, since our trust is being so consistently betrayed.

Blockchain removes the need to trust a centralized

middleman—whether it's a brand, a company, or an institution—with your data. It's a way to enable self-sovereign identity, which simply means the ability to keep control over your personal and business data. With blockchain, users control what that data is, how it's stored, and when and how it gets used.

In blockchain-based Web 3.0, users will also have the right to say what will be done with their data, that is, the data collected on them. Power and control are being put back in the hands of individuals on a truly peer-to-peer basis, bypassing intermediaries. You'll now be able to network with others without revealing your data to third parties.

With blockchain, you don't need to trust a bank and pay all its fees to make a transaction or send money from one place to another. Blockchain's cryptographic mechanisms enable you to have truly peer-to-peer interactions on global networks that are as large or small in scale as appropriate.

In a sense, the evolution of Web 3.0 involves a move back to the peer-to-peer environment of such early Web 1.0 use cases as email, while maintaining the scope and convenience of Web 2.0 networking. It's the best of both worlds. To take another example, you won't need to rely on centralized platforms such as Netflix or Spotify to access movies or streaming music. You'll be able to access the latest songs by your favorite musicians by owning and transferring a utility token that gives you the right to such access. The financial benefits of the token will then be paid out not to intermediaries, but to the musicians themselves.

UNDER CONSTRUCTION

The infrastructure for all this is just starting to be built at present, just as the Web 1.0 infrastructure was being built in 1994. A phone was a phone in 1994, not a computer, bank, and camera you were able to hold in your hand. Blockchain-based networks are beginning to go live and come online. The tools to make blockchains more usable and enable blockchain interoperability are currently under construction.

We're on the cusp, and there's going to be an adoption curve. This is not going to happen overnight. Blockchain is the next phase of networking, and it's almost as if the infrastructure we're familiar with from Web 1.0 and Web 2.0 is being rebuilt.

The clear user expectation is that Web 3.0 services will work as elegantly and seamlessly, and be as usable, as Web 2.0 services are now. We're still quite a ways from that goal. At this point, blockchains are admittedly hard to use. They're slow—significantly slower than Facebook or the Visa network. Why, then, are so many people investing the time, money, and resources to build decentralized, blockchain-based applications, tools, and infrastructure?

Of course, there's the privacy issue, which is vital and increasingly being seen as such. Another fundamental Web 3.0 thesis is that the next networking cycle will involve important innovations in business models that move away from data ownership and trading in user data. What could networking become if data weren't a commodity, but exchanged either freely or solely at users' discretion and with their consent? This is a higher-level concept than blockchain itself, which is why the term Web 3.0 is so useful.

One threshold or inflection point occurred about five years ago with the advent and increasing importance of machine learning or AI systems. These involve a shift away from data siloed in separate databases into a more open and connected system. All this is now beginning to bring monopolistic data ownership as the core internet business model into question.

A BUSINESS-MODEL SHIFT

In the history of media—and the web is certainly, among other things, a communications medium—there hasn't been all that much business-model innovation. Newspapers, radio, and television all made money through advertising. When the internet came about, it seemed logical to apply these older industries' business models to what was fundamentally a new paradigm.

The problem is that the advertising business model led us to where we are today. To make money through advertising, companies need to collect and own user data, so it can be sold to advertisers and their brokers. Today's huge Web 2.0 companies work because they have become data monopolies.

Web 3.0 marks a shift in the paradigm, in that we're innovating not just on the technological, but on the business-model level. Blockchain is truly transformative, because it allows transactions to take place on a truly peer-to-peer basis, bypassing middlemen.

We can now start to think about what this implies. What can we build? What sorts of businesses and business models can be created to share and exchange value between the creators of a product or service and the people consuming it? Looking beyond business models, how do we create balanced economic incentives that help us reframe how we think about work and business in the first place?

More and more people—so-called users—are realizing

the pitfalls of the current situation. The big Web 2.0 companies are harvesting their data in trade for distraction and entertainment. It's an unhealthy situation when Facebook or a similar company innovates, or so it seems, primarily in order to increase its users' addictions.

Certainly, the leaders of these companies, profit as they may, know something is wrong. Silicon Valley big shots don't want their kids spending all their time on smartphones using the products they're building. These are very intelligent people who, you would think, might want to use that intelligence to create new business models that could make them a lot of money in a more principled fashion.

Of course, there's a purely mercenary side to human nature, but there's also a side that wants to improve, enhance, and build upon what's already been done. Blockchain is a technology serving, in my opinion, as a catalyst for this type of change. The underlying paradigm shift is from centralized and siloed to decentralized and open data.

This was already beginning to happen on a cultural level, and the technology followed. Satoshi Nakamoto's bitcoin white paper came along just at a time when events made people very distrustful of the global banking system. Bitcoin and blockchain seemed to provide a solution. That's why bitcoin has persisted. It's more an idea and religion than a technology. Now people are using and building on the technology, but again it's still in its very early stages.

Since the time of Satoshi's white paper, we've experienced countless data hacks and leaks, including high-profile incidents involving Equifax, Facebook, and Starwood Hotels. We've been through countless foodborne outbreaks, such as E. coli at Chipotle, as well as tainted lettuce, cereal, and you name it. We've been subjected to fake news and seen governments use social media to manipulate elections. Consumers are beginning to see the genuine value of decentralization.

THE ORIGIN STORY

Let's take a historical perspective like Warren Buffett would and look back to the banner year of 1994. The launch of Windows 95 that year was one among multiple user-friendly operating systems. More significantly, 1994 was the year the Netscape Navigator browser was introduced.

As mentioned earlier, what we call the internet was originally designed by DARPA, the US military's research arm, as a decentralized communications network relatively immune to attack. For decades, it was used by specialists in the government and academia who had the computer and programming skills required.

English scientist Tim Berners-Lee developed a means of accessing the information available on the internet through hyperlinks in 1989, creating what was known as the World Wide Web. He released the first web browser in 1990. It wasn't until 1994, however, that Netscape introduced the first truly usable browser and what is now called Web 1.0 became accessible to the general public.

In 1996, Microsoft released a competitive browser, the Internet Explorer (IE), launching the browser wars. IE definitely won the first round, largely because it was incorporated into every copy of the Windows operating system. Of course, many different browsers have been developed since then, and IE itself is now something of a historical curiosity.

What's more important is that we now think about browsers mainly in hindsight. They've fallen into the background. We rarely if ever even think about the fact that we're using a browser as our window onto the web. It's become a utility. In 1994, however, this was all new to most people. They were still trying to get their heads around what the web was, just like we're doing with blockchain now. Was it a global information library? An encyclopedia that could somehow be accessed through the phone line? How were we going to find what we were looking for? Access speeds, generally via telephone lines, were also much slower than they have since become.

BUILDING WEB 3.0

Of course, Web 3.0 is being built in a very different environment, within the context of the now twenty-five-year history of popular internet use. Along the way, the overall web infrastructure-and-applications development cycle has led to e-commerce, online communities, and many different connectivity modes.

Web 3.0 is still at the "early browser" stage. Scalability challenges need to be resolved, just as they had to be resolved during the early days of Web 1.0. We're only starting to be able to process blockchain-enabled transactions and are just beginning to see the advent of decentralized apps. These are like early browsers in that they are new ways to interact on and with the networks that will eventually serve as vehicles for mass adoption.

It's still unclear, really, what the key tools in the still-unwritten history of blockchain will be. A lot of both Web 1.0 and Web 2.0's value is tied up in the network's application services layers, which are the basis of web-based businesses. The value of blockchain is, in contrast, tied up in more fundamental protocol layers.

Tim Berners-Lee's World Wide Web, which is still basically the web we use today, was built on a single protocol: hyper-text transfer protocol, or http. There are many, many competing protocols underlying Web 3.0, which is where blockchain-enabled transactions take place and there is money to be made.

Web 3.0 protocols also bear a functional resemblance to Web 1.0 browsers. There will probably be protocol wars similar to the early browser wars. Some protocols are going to win, some are going to lose, and some that persist may be tightly linked to specific use cases. What's going to happen is anyone's guess at the moment.

LESSONS FROM THE DOT-COM BUBBLE

In the late nineties, things got crazy. Internet companies proliferated, many built on little more than poorly thought-through business models. Wall Street went nuts, driving up valuations of many companies—"dot-coms"—that had little or no intrinsic value. What happened was a classic bubble, and the so-called dot-com bubble burst at the turn of the millennium.

The reaction to all this was as shortsighted as what had come before. Suddenly, the web was washed out, at least in the financial sector, even though it was clear to most in the industry, even those who had just lost their jobs, that the underlying technology was sound and would continue to grow in importance.

What's important to look at in all this is the nature of

adoption curves, which will also be critical in the rise of Web 3.0. Amazon's stock was highly valued before the bubble burst—when it was still just an online book and music store—and then fell to eight dollars a share. It took the company seven years to get its stock back up to the level it had been at before the bust, much less to grow to where it is today as the massive cloud-computing, e-commerce, and AI behemoth it is. Web 3.0 is still in the early years of building products for niche markets. It has yet to grow beyond its baby steps.

Since many Web 1.0 business models weren't rooted in anything substantial, they were knocked over by the first strong wind. There's something to be learned here about building infrastructure responsibly. However, people aren't always responsible, to put it mildly, and when something balloons into a trend or fad, it's often party time.

THE 2017 BOOM

For blockchain, 2017 was a banner year. The reason was the introduction of Ethereum's ERC-20 protocol, which led to a proliferation of ICOs (initial coin offerings) with strong resemblance to the proliferation of dot-coms in the late nineties. Something significant had been created, and people found a way to exploit it, as they tend to do.

Suddenly, there was another boom. Literally everyone

I talked to was now a blockchain expert. The first mainstream media coverage hit, with CNBC running the equivalent of an ICO token-price stock ticker. The hike in mainstream awareness made everything crazier.

I'd overhear Uber drivers on the phone with their friends, telling them how to buy Ether. When everyone starts talking about something, you know it's a bubble. True, a lot of people used the ICO mechanism to raise money with the best of intentions, to build a product or infrastructure. There were plenty of scams as well.

As we've seen, the SEC has since started to provide guidance—better late than never. Many challenges in the regulatory landscape still need to be resolved, especially in the United States, where a more stringent approach to ICOs is now being taken, although countries in other parts of the world have embraced them. Again, it's still early days.

Some ICOs were clearly irresponsible scams that used blockchain networks' anonymity to bilk investors. People go nuts when a lot of money is being raised overnight. By the end of 2017, bitcoin, the original cryptocurrency, ran up to an all-time high, breaking $20,000.

Some people suddenly became crypto-millionaires or billionaires. They weren't necessarily doing anything wrong. They just had bought bitcoin early. The peak of the bull market led to Wolf-of-Wall-Street lifestyles, with people throwing lavish parties in remote castles in France or buying and showing off Lamborghinis. Why Lamborghinis? Lambos, as they became known, were a luxury car brand you could buy directly with bitcoin, which many did, because they provided bitcoin holdings with a measure of liquidity not available elsewhere.

However, Web 2.0 social network companies aren't immune to indulgent lifestyles, either. Look at the corporate headquarters of some of the big companies in Silicon Valley and San Francisco, and the extreme lengths they've gone to, offering daily catered lunches, doggy daycare, laundry services, and lavish holiday parties. The HBO series *Silicon Valley* provides spot-on satire of the phenomenon.

There was also the "use case," mentioned in the last chapter, of people spending ridiculous amounts of money just to get into crypto conferences, most of which have now shut down. A tremendous shift moved investment away from traditional markets. Know-nothing investors were buying tokens in order, as Warren Buffett pointed out toward the end of the bubble, to speculate for speculation's sake.

This led to a run-up in prices. Then a lot of people got

screwed, just like when the dot-com bubble burst. Even people who, at the height of the bubble, weren't investing in ICOs, but in bitcoin, which is relatively safe in the grand scheme of things, saw their investments go down 80 percent.

BEYOND THE BOOM

In 2017, a lot of people raised a lot of money. They spent it on lifestyles that did not involve building products, infrastructure, or tools. Yet plenty of other people were actually building products and infrastructure and continue to do so. You just didn't hear about them in the media.

Now, we've shifted back into a bear market and are on the flip side, just like in 2001. Companies have folded or laid off 70 percent of their workforce.

The point is that there are parallels to 1994, as well as to 2001. To repeat yet again: it's still early. Many people don't think that Web 3.0 has hit the 1999 mark yet, and that in a few years there will be another run-up as the next phase of the infrastructure is built. Any time we hit a bull market in the cycle, there's more exposure, and more newbies or "tourists" become aware of, and invest in, the hot new thing. The good thing about such investment is that it also helps products get built, which makes it easier to access the network.

Web 3.0 is being built by people who believe in the technology and its potential. These are the people who are working on real businesses and real business models. Let's look at what they've already started doing.

CHAPTER 11

DEMAND CHAINS: A NEW, BLOCKCHAIN-ENABLED WAY OF DOING BUSINESS

In the early twentieth century, scrappy upstart restaurant chains blazed their way into an entirely new frontier of business-model generation. Until then, most restaurants were small, local, and often family owned. Their processes were inconsistent, quality variable, and suppliers engaged with handshake deals.

In 1923, Roy W. Allen and Frank Wright opened the first fast-food restaurant, A&W. By 1926, it had evolved into a franchise. In the 1950s and 1960s, there was a massive boom in restaurant franchising, exemplified by McDonald's.

After World War II, America was quite literally booming. Suburbs cropped up almost everywhere, and eating habits were changing. Sociocultural and technological innovations such as the rise of the automobile and the interstate highway system created an environment ripe for innovation. Television supplanted radio as the focus of home entertainment, and eating habits also shifted with both "TV dinners" and the fast-food explosion.

I could continue to tell you a story of almost insane growth and scale, of greed and deception, and of cheeseburgers and Coca-Cola in American food history.

But I won't.

Why? Because I'm assuming many of you have seen the movie *The Founder* and know the story of the McDonald brothers, the Big Mac, and Ray Kroc, the man who made McDonald's what it is today. They standardized and made production more efficient while applying a franchising concept, a business model that had been around for centuries.

Yet the McDonald's story is simply one of recombinant innovation.

Since this book is about Pizza, I'd like to tell you a different, bigger story. A story about the world's largest Pizza chain, a company that does tens of billions in global sales and whose stock regularly outperforms Amazon, Apple, Netflix, and Alphabet (Google).

Domino's Pizza.

Before I lose you to ordering some Pizza with your bit-coin—I promise you'll get it at the end of the book—let's talk about Domino's, which, in my humble opinion, is one of the most successful technology companies of our time. You heard that right: technology company.

In the 2000s, Domino's became one of the first compa-nies to introduce an online Pizza tracker, one of the best supply-chain-track-and-trace and real-time logistics tools I've ever seen. Domino's went on to offer a virtual voice assistant in its app, and enabled Twitter ordering, Pizza delivery drones in New Zealand, and even augmented-reality billboards that accept orders. Beyond these marketing initiatives, Domino's has launched a purpose-built vehicle called the Domino's Delivery Expert (DXP) equipped with space for eighty Pizzas and a warming station. More recently, it has partnered with Ford to test autonomous delivery vehicles.

Let's go back to the very beginning of this book. Remem-ber Zume Pizza? The company that is actually cooking Pizzas on demand in mobile, modular, autonomous delivery vehicles? Good. You can see how in even the most mundane of industries—not so mundane when you realize Pizza accounts for 61 percent of the total delivery market[1]—radical evolution can occur.[2]

The question is: what blockchain-based business models can we expect? Business models that aren't simply examples of recombinant innovation, digital transformation, or whatever other strategy-consulting buzzword you want to throw in here.

This is where innovation gets really exciting and more speculative, although it's already possible to see progress being made. The focus so far has been on blockchain's role in secure, disintermediated financial transactions. Cryptocurrency was the first blockchain use case. However, any business model involves a transaction of goods and services and almost always has a financial component.

How can blockchain transform the transactions involved in innovative business models? The potential is already clear, but how that potential will be realized involves making predictions, which is both an intriguing and dangerous process.

Who could have predicted, in its early days, that Facebook would not only win the social network wars but have the

---

1   NPD Group, "Cowen Delivery Survey," 2018, Cowen and Company.

2   We're leaving buzzwords like "radical innovation" and "digital transformation" at the door.

profound impact it's now had in so many different areas? Could anyone have foreseen that what started out as a way to rate college women would come to influence elections all over the globe?

It's doubtful Mark Zuckerberg knew at the time what he was building, although he has certainly been diligent about seizing the opportunities that have presented themselves. Even visionaries are unable to predict what will happen when you first plant a seed.

THE EVOLUTION OF SUPPLY CHAINS

What I call "demand chains"—a concept MIT's Michael Casey also discusses—are a perfect example of how blockchain technology can make entirely new business models possible. Supply chains are themselves networks whose very nature globalization has transformed in recent decades. Demand chains are essentially supply chains from which blockchain technology can remove links no longer necessary as we become an even more global society. This will yield many collateral economic, sociocultural, and geopolitical benefits.

My father's business was in retail and became involved in a number of different products: toys, patio equipment, chemicals, and so on. His company was one of the first, back in the eighties, to outsource offshore manufacturing to China. This was early in the trend of connecting with overseas firms to scale production, which coincided with the advent of the computerization of inventory management and other large-scale business processes.

I spent many weekends playing hide-and-seek in warehouses, riding on forklifts, and playing with a really nifty coffee-vending machine that actually dropped a cup and poured coffee all at once—don't worry, the ten-year-old me was drinking hot chocolate. I stood in awe of the massive IBM mainframe computers running the whole show, from inventory, to automated sorting, to the trucks in the loading dock. It was like magic. I guess you could say I come from a long line of obsessive systems thinkers.

If we've now entered the so-called fourth industrial revolution, with machine learning, AI, and other transformative technologies such as blockchain, the advances my father's company was involved in were part of the third industrial revolution of digitization and globalization— although I'd be the first to say that he was way ahead of his time. The first two industrial revolutions—based first on steam and then on electricity—took us from artisans making craft products with local materials to large-scale mass production and automation. The third industrial revolution was made possible by the development of the vast communication networks that made global logistics possible.

The world today consists of immense global supply chains that are often quite complicated and confusing. To begin with, they were more efficient than what came before, which seems almost incredible. Now they've gotten so complex that they've become riddled with new problems and challenges. Hundreds of materials and components from all over the world go into making an iPhone. Countries of origin impose tariffs on materials, and the countries in which the product is assembled are often half a world away from where they are sold. This makes controlling authenticity and quality challenging, with gray markets enabling counterfeit and diverted products to enter the supply chain.

In recent years, some manufacturers have focused on vertical integration as a way of meeting the challenges of this complexity. A number of direct-to-consumer brands have popped up. When launching its business, Warby Parker took a close look at and analyzed the supply-chain logistics of Luxottica Group, the world's largest manufacturer of eyeglasses and frames. By eliminating some of the links in the chain—some of the vendors—through vertical integration, they were able to offer glasses to consumers at a significantly lower cost, while continuing to preserve margins similar to Luxottica's and making a comparable per-unit profit. It was probably even more valuable that they owned the relationship with their customers. They were producer, brand, and retailer simultaneously.

This model has been extensively replicated for products of all kinds, such as luggage, shoes, and Casper mattresses. In my opinion, this is as good as it's going to get in terms of optimizing traditional supply chains. And this is still a suboptimal solution to the problems being faced and the issues at stake.

Another example of vertical integration is Harry's, the direct-to-consumer razor company. They put themselves in competition with Gillette, whose business model involves a very traditional supply chain. Harry's made a point of meeting and talking with razor component manufacturers. It turns out that there aren't that many, and most were completely beholden to, although not owned by, Gillette. Harry's had to raise about $120 million in private equity funding to buy its own razor factory.

That was their solution. After understanding how monopolistic and complicated the current system was, Harry's decided they needed to own their own production. While the approach made business sense, it couldn't be called innovative.

COMBINING THE LOCAL WITH THE GLOBAL

The next, far more innovative phase, I passionately believe, will be built on the assumption of continuing globalization, global connections, and global brands, but will be significantly different from the current fragmented supply-chain approach. For example, people from all over the world want to buy products from brands that are based in New York. While there will always be local crafts, we're never going to go back to a system entirely founded on production from local artisans. What will emerge instead will be a combination of the local and the global.

This won't occur by consolidating the factory model. Henry Ford's assembly line was an innovation at the time. All the competitors who didn't adopt his production model were put out of business within twenty years, but that was over a century ago. It seems a little crazy to further automate and network a production and supply-chain system that is essentially outdated.

Blockchain can address certain fundamental flaws and inefficiencies in the current supply-chain system. Let's say it has cost General Electric (GE) millions of dollars to design a jet airplane engine part. The way things work today, an original equipment manufacturer (OEM) like GE will mass-produce such parts in one location, where they can manage production, compliance, and quality. These parts are then sent around the world to airports or maintenance facilities, where they sit on shelves as inventory. The same goes for auto parts, food, clothing, and pretty much anything you might buy or consume.

Blockchain, combined with technologies such as additive manufacturing, can flip this model on its head. It can not only save GE and other companies millions of dollars by eliminating logistical leapfrogging but ensure higher-quality products that haven't been sitting on shelves. Blockchain can eliminate inventory costs and risk, and contribute to sustainability by preventing companies from overproducing.

But there's a catch. GE is not going to put the design file for its airplane-engine part into a database so that 3-D printing machines can manufacture it in every airport in the world. They need and have a right to protect their intellectual property (IP). The part did cost hundreds of millions to design, after all.

The design file could, however, be placed in a blockchain, rendering the IP secure and trust unnecessary. Each time the part needs replacing, the design file could be unlocked directly from the industrial 3-D printer and the part manufactured at the airport where a replacement is needed. GE gets paid for its IP, which remains secure and is unlocked again the next time a replacement part is needed.

This just-in-time, localized production is such a radical departure from today's norms that it may seem as imprac-tical as science fiction. However, this approach also solves a number of existing problems without creating new ones. For one thing, the part is not being overproduced. Mass production often equates to overproduction and leads to inventory risk, one of the biggest sticking points of the current supply-chain system.

The way to solve the problem is not through more computing, more machine intelligence or AI, and more planning. The very literal solution is to make things as they are needed through just-in-time or on-demand production, turning supply chains into far more efficient and cost-effective demand chains.

Think of the innovative business models this approach would enable in many different industries and verticals, such as apparel and agriculture. Products would be ordered and delivered on an as-needed basis. Instead of building huge factories in remote locations, the products would be manufactured relatively locally, cutting down on shipping costs. You might think of this as a very innovative method of drop-shipping.

Once established, this approach could successfully compete with Amazon Prime two-day delivery. Out-of-stock issues are still encountered when ordering from Amazon, because Amazon still deals with vast networks of production and distribution centers. While Amazon has done an excellent job of supply-chain optimization, there's always a better way to do things, especially in technologically transformative times like the present.

DEFINING DEMAND CHAINS

Let's analyze and define demand chains more precisely. Today's supply chains are vast and convoluted global networks with materials and products coming in and going out. Any supply chain is also a value chain, in that each link in the chain, if it is to remain viable, must add value to the process or network as a whole.

Generally speaking, the links in a demand chain will add far greater value than links in today's global supply chains. As many extraneous, intermediary links in the chain as possible can and will be eliminated: wholesalers, inventory storage, distributors, and retailers. The chain will be collapsed by eliminating as many middlemen as possible. Demand-chain networks will also include localized manufacturing centers capable of producing one, ten thousand, or even a million units of a product on demand and as needed.

Blockchain technology makes this possible by again enabling direct peer-to-peer connection. Its first use case has, of course, been in financial services, where it has shown itself capable of innovating by providing direct, secure exchanges between seller and buyer or producer and consumer.

Most industries today are focused on dealing with inefficiencies, as opposed to solving for or eliminating them. Most of these inefficiencies are caused by fragmentation, specialization, and intermediaries that benefit from existing supply chains, but are not intrinsically necessary to the basic transactions involved.

What's been missing is trust or, more accurately, no longer needing trust. In the present system, no one is going to trust Google to share its intellectual property or Amazon to do on-demand 3-D printing manufacturing. Blockchain solves that problem. It's the previously missing piece of the puzzle of how to disentangle today's enormous global supply chains.

Demand chains lead to circular economies aimed at minimizing waste and maximizing the use of resources. Current supply chains raise significant, worrisome sustainability issues, including the exploitation of natural resources and the environment, and the working conditions in large factories. Some of this comes about through logistical inefficiencies and the need to ship things all over the world. Some of it comes from packaging inefficiencies or the need for packaging in the first place. Other inefficiencies, such as the overuse of raw materials, must also be factored in.

We're not just getting to, but are already past a tipping point of needing to be more mindful of our resources. We've started sending spaceships to asteroids to mine minerals and metals, but that hardly seems the most effective approach. A demand-based model is capable of eliminating much of the waste the current system creates.

Apparel companies like H&M are a perfect example. Many of them now go through fifty-two "fast fashion" design-and-manufacturing cycles a year. Fashions now change once every week! Each one of those cycles creates volumes of unbought and unused clothing inventory that is burned or thrown into landfills. All of this is done in the name of maintaining brand value. That goal may be achieved, but at what price?

A shift in consumption behaviors is occurring in response, especially among younger demographics. There are now circular-economy clothing companies where you can return your old clothes instead of donating them to an organization where they often remain unused. The clothes are shredded down to the threads, out of which new garments are created right there, on the spot. The ultimate value of this may be debatable, but the same principle is applied to waste management, recycling plastic that can then be repurposed and reused or not producing new plastic in the first place.

Single-use plastics account for 50 percent or more of all plastic waste, and most single-use plastics are found in our grocery store aisles. As we move to more localized food production with blockchain-connected vertical farms closer to the cities they serve, or even to connecting and incentivizing peer-to-peer backyard farmers, we eliminate the need for packaging and shipping altogether.

Since resources are finite, it seems natural, in all senses of the word, to develop sustainable technologies and circular economies. Demand chains are a key element here, since they bring the endpoints of supply and demand so much closer together, making the chain into a circle. That's not the way we've been operating up until now.

I was talking with an acquaintance who runs a denim mill based in Pakistan, and he said that there was so much excess production that the mill had to shut down and lay off seven thousand people. The reason was that, with the rise of fast fashion, margins have gotten so thin that brands are going to the factory and saying, "You're making this for four dollars. We need it for two dollars." The factory can't do it. Nobody can. The factories start operating at a loss and inevitably close down.

If consumers expect their clothes to be cheaper, we need to find new ways to cut down margins, other than basically just screwing the producer—and our planet. The only way this can be done is to cut out the links in the middle of the supply chain—all the logistics and all the markups. The demand chain needs to go from the producer, the network, or distributed manufacturing network directly to the consumer.

Again, we're talking about a genuine paradigm shift in manufacturing, just as we were in finance. Blockchain technology is significant, I feel, in terms both of its underlying capabilities and its ability to get people started thinking about new models, particularly distributed business models. Theoretically, it enables us to think of new ways of doing things, and then, technologically, it enables those new models to be put into practice.

LOCAL AND JUST-IN-TIME

Start from the premise of allowing the intellectual property of an essentially infinite number of brands to coexist on a blockchain network without fear of piracy. Then imagine how retail might evolve from this. Massive shopping malls—which, however large, are finite spaces for storing the finite inventory of a finite number of brands— could be replaced by community-focused retail centers whose footprint might only be twice as large as the typical Starbucks.

Customers could tap into such a retail center either physically or virtually and order anything in a robust Sears Roebuck- or Amazon-like catalog. The product would then be produced right there on demand. In some cases, the demand chain might not extend all the way down to the point of sale. Perhaps a modular facility would produce items on demand and hand them over to local couriers or ride-share drivers. There will be no longer be a need for a wholesaler to buy items from a factory, marking them up and sending them down the supply chain in which every link demands its cut, meaning the customer pays more.

Connecting consumers directly to producers would have enormous benefits: restoring trust and eliminating the need for baseless certifications and third-party audits; restoring brand loyalty; restoring the environment, which has suffered the massive consequences of industrialization; and restoring community and connection with ourselves, each other, and the products we consume.

A blockchain capable of protecting and licensing brand or product IP has other implications. Blockchain technology would enable smart contracts specifying, for example, that each time a T-shirt is bought, 20 percent of the price goes to the brand as a royalty, a certain percentage goes to the retail outlet or point of sale, a certain percentage goes to the owner of the 3-D printer that manufactured the shirt, and another to the worker who operated the printer. The system would be rationalized rather than cumulative. This is much the same system that could now enable royalties to be paid directly from a buyer to artists or musicians, the creators or producers of a graphic design or a song.

All this involves new automated modes of production, including robots as well as 3-D printers. In this "machine economy," part of the product's cost will need to go to maintaining the machines themselves. In a blockchain network, each 3-D printer, for instance, could have its own identity and a wallet or piggy bank enabling it to pay for its own repairs and maintenance. This is an idea that's no longer crazy or even very far off.

Autonomous vehicles will serve as test cases for these systems. A self-driving car on a blockchain network could have its own wallet that accepts payment from the rider. Some of the payment goes to the company, such as Uber or a decentralized collective, that owns the car, and some remains with the car, which then goes and makes its own payments at a charging station. Machine learning, or AI, technology is being built that will allow the car to make the decisions necessary to manage its piggy bank.

This may seem like a futuristic fantasy, but it's happening now. Blockchain allows both people and machines to have wallets, which is to say, automated ways of making payments, including micropayments, and other transactions.

The payment trail in a supply chain involves complicated accounting and bookkeeping. A demand trail has a far simpler financial structure: one percentage to the brand, another for materials, and yet another for manufacturing. The blockchain can also easily handle changes to these figures in cases of renegotiation. Blockchains are incredibly useful in bringing communities and ecosystems together, because they enable self-maintaining networks of any size to be built on a peer-to-peer basis that bypasses the need for trust.

Blockchains didn't need to incorporate 3-D printing technology in the financial sector but can do so in the case of on-demand manufacturing. Initially, 3-D printing allowed production of small amounts of plastic or, later, metal parts, and much of its application was in the aerospace and automotive industries. The technology has now been developed to the point that 3-D printing can produce up to one hundred thousand units of an item more cheaply than overseas injection molding. We can 3-D print anything from a jet engine part to a T-shirt, to a lab-grown protein burger, to a human heart. And that's only the beginning.

My company Chronicled did an early luxury goods–

authentication project that required microchip-enabled hang tags. If we had decided to go the injection-molding route, we would have spent between $10,000 and $20,000 to create the tooling for the complex disc into which the chip had to be inserted. After creating the tooling, we would have had to wait six to eight weeks for production, been forced to meet a hundred-thousand-unit minimum, and, to make things worse, we wouldn't have been able to change the design. This is why many hardware companies die in the prototyping graveyard. They cannot iterate and incorporate feedback as quickly as nimbler software companies can.

Instead, we manufactured the tags just-in-time through 3-D printing. The quality of 3-D printers these days has moved from prototyping to production quality. Post-processing is minimal or even nonexistent. It's price-competitive with mass manufacturing, even for high volumes. Printers can print anything from plastics and metals to organs and food.

ON-DEMAND PRODUCTION

Now 3-D-printing machines can create complex objects optimized with respect to the materials used. There are also AI programs that can help optimize on cost by minimizing the amount of materials used in manufacturing a product. These industrial printing machines cost hundreds of thousands of dollars until recently, much like early mainframe computers did. Now they're coming down in cost and size and being commoditized. I doubt we'll ever see 3-D printer laptops in everyone's home, if only because of the materials needed to do manufacturing, but they are becoming far more accessible to a wider variety of manufacturers.

Comparable technologies are being applied to agriculture. All these innovations are converging on creating products with smaller footprints based on local demand. Rather than growing tons of tomatoes in some remote locale, spraying them, preserving them, and shipping them all over the world, a vertical farm can grow organic tomatoes hydroponically in greenhouses or repurposed warehouses for strictly local consumption.

So many innovative business models could be based on on-demand production that it's not a question of whether this will happen. It certainly will, if only for basic economic reasons, with markets needing to become increasingly efficient. The question is: when? It's hard to predict. Five years? Ten years? The shift from supply to demand chains is not going to be an easy one, given the self-interest of the powers that be and everyone who benefits from the current infrastructure.

Personally, however, I'm tired of retrofitting supply

chains. My interest is in building the future, not fixing the past.[3] The good news is the shift we're seeing on the cryptocurrency side. Bitcoin and blockchain involved shifting away from institutions, yet now institutional investors have become interested and are getting involved. The attitude has become: if you can't beat 'em, join 'em.

To think about how the blockchain-technology paradigm shift is going to affect the future, look at the first use case, the financial industry, and extrapolate. Again, the biggest potential of blockchain technology is its impact on business models, and this may affect every industry and vertical globally, aside from having major political and trade implications.

Blockchain technology will fundamentally change how we transact, how we live, and how we share things. People will be incentivized in new ways to perform activities and tasks and to exchange value in new ways and may not necessarily work for just one company with just one salary. People will learn and earn from many sources, continuously. When I think about the potential of blockchain for the future of work and education, I can see how they and we are all going to be transformed.

---

3   Well, at least fixing the mistakes of the past by building the future!

CHAPTER 12

UNLOCKING BIG DATA: BETTER CALL BLOCKCHAIN!

At sixteen years old, I was a typical high school student: I studied, played sports, participated in theater. One day, while at lacrosse practice doing a timed hundred-meter run, I dropped to the ground. Just like that. Unconscious and without a pulse. My heart was beating—well, fluttering—at over 450 beats per minute, high enough to be considered a flatline. I was revived—obviously, since I'm still here to write this book!—but the next few months were a whirlwind.

After being rushed to the ER and shocked back into life with a defibrillator, I was hooked up to a portable device called a halter monitor that would record my heart's activity and trigger a notification if it was stopping again. The problem was, the monitor was clunky—about the size of a laptop—and I had wires all over my body. Also, it was a manual device, so if the heart problem recurred and I went unconscious, someone would need to call my cardiologist on the phone and play him the sound-wave version of my heartbeat. Not very advanced technology, if you ask me.

Within a few days, the monitor picked up another event that occurred while I was sleeping. After I woke up, my parents called in the readings, and shortly thereafter I was in the hospital for surgery. All I remember was the surgical team blasting music in the operating room: Billy Joel's "My Life." It was so quirky, weird, and laughable. Or maybe that was the sedatives they gave me.

To make a long story short, they burned away some accessory pathways that were causing the short-circuiting. And voilà! Fixed!

Last year, I had a checkup with my cardiologist and was amazed to see that the monitor I'd be wearing for two weeks this time around was about the size of a quail egg. It stuck right to my chest and was hardly noticeable.

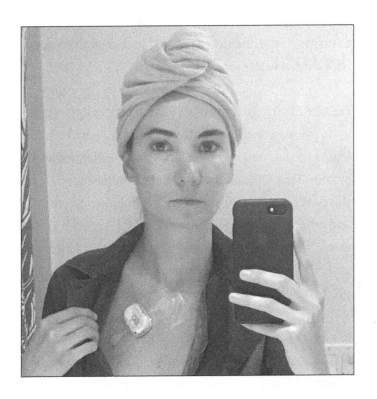

More recently, I read an article about the new Apple Watch. Its monitor is able to detect abnormal heart rates—arrhythmia, supraventricular tachycardia, atrial fibrillation, ventricular tachycardia—and a range of other conditions. If the watch detects an abnormality, it will send you a notification.

This is an interesting and powerful advance in sensor technology. But there is still the challenge of where all of the data collected is going and how it is shared. How can it be shared with the right parties, such as your doctor, to ensure better healthcare? And how do you ensure it isn't shared with the wrong parties?

We already live in a world of big data that all the digital systems we constantly interact with collect. Machine learning—sometimes called artificial intelligence or AI—systems have and will continue to be developed to analyze this data for patterns that then can be applied to business and other decisions. The amount of data is already far too overwhelming for people to analyze, although professionals will continue to evaluate machine-learning-generated predictions before deciding whether to apply them.

We ain't seen nothing yet! The amount of available data will increase exponentially with the growth of sensor technology and the so-called Internet of Things (IoT), in which data-collecting sensors will be built into many, if not most, of our appliances and other devices. The use case most often cited, to the point of cliché, is the IoT refrigerator, which can tell when you are low on milk and then order another gallon to be delivered by conventional carriers, or, in the near future, by drone. Beyond smart devices, sensors are now cheaper and smaller than ever, some the size of a grain of rice. They will be everywhere: from tiny sensors sprayed on crops to measure soil quality to bio-sensors in our bloodstream looking for cancerous cells.

Where does blockchain fit in? Blockchain technology

is one important, but far from the only, critical techno-logical advance in what is being called both the "fourth industrial revolution" and Web 3.0. Blockchain will not only interoperate with these other technologies, but be a critical factor enabling such interoperability. Again, this process's many potential benefits coexist with a dysto-pian dimension. Looking at the issues brought about by "too much data," a number of examples from both sides of the spectrum will emerge.

SECURE DATA EXCHANGE

On a theoretical level, Web 3.0 comprises a shift from current data silos and strict data ownership to more open data exchange on blockchain-enabled networks, which is made possible by blockchain's ability to verify data with-out giving away the store. The result is that companies previously unwilling to share data and build interoperable systems will now be able to do so.

Let's take an example with both clearly beneficial and possibly dystopian effects. At one point, I had the oppor-tunity to speak to a number of insurance companies about a use case in the pharmaceutical industry involv-ing a vertical market that my company Chronicled has worked with to help control the opioid epidemic. This is a major American health crisis, and it would seem that anything that might be done to turn back the tide of opioid addiction would have a net benefit in terms of lives saved.

Pharmacies already track information about the nature and number of prescriptions people are filling, especially for opioids like Oxycontin. Red-flag alerts for potential addictive behavior can be generated and sent to health plans or insurers. However, this doesn't solve the problem that arises when a spouse or significant other has a different health plan, enabling an addict to obtain more Oxycontin by other means. The data about you and your spouse is siloed, and the two insurance companies involved aren't sharing the information.

Blockchain technology enables this data to be taken out of a silo and shared between competing health plans, with alerts and interventions generated from a data pool. Blockchain protects the security of the data, while enabling machine-learning analysis capable of giving a more complete picture than now possible.

Health plans see this approach as a public good, and it is, in fact, a way of monitoring a problem that has turned into a plague in many parts of the country. However, a Big Brother-ish aspect to all this needs to be acknowledged and will need to be dealt with. We must be diligent in preventing the use of this and other emerging technologies from supporting an autocratic surveillance state. All tools can be weapons if wielded the wrong way.

IOT

With the Internet of Things—from now on we'll use the common abbreviation, IoT—the number of web-connected devices and the data they generate will increase exponentially. Many people aren't aware that not only the cost, but the size of sensors has gone way down. Microsensors in the soil, the size of an aerosol spray, are tracking crop information. Aside from smart refrigerators, there are smart toasters, smart TVs, and smart whatevers. People wear Fitbits, AirPods, and medical devices capable of tracking physiological data: heartbeat, number of steps taken in a day, blood pressure, and much more. There is sensor data—including that gathered by Alexa and similar home devices—on almost every aspect of our lives. The data may be very broad, quite specific, or anywhere in between.

Many different companies build and sell these sensor devices. Each company stores the data its devices collect in its own databases. Blockchain will enable all this IoT data to be put into a shared ledger constituting an unimaginably massive dataset. Machine learning or artificial intelligence algorithms are able to analyze and find patterns in datasets of this size, and they also require huge datasets to be properly trained. The whole process is a huge positive-feedback loop.

For years, IBM was in a business phase focused on amassing huge datasets. They are now building machine learning and AI systems, like Watson, trained with this data, which are becoming one of their biggest product lines.

How big the impact of all this will be is still unknown, but it's called the fourth industrial revolution for a reason. Blockchain is a technology not for storing, but for unlocking the potential of all this data and, most importantly, for trusting its veracity. Veracity and integrity are critical because we don't want to be training our AIs on faulty datasets. The results might be catastrophic.

When I was training as a private pilot, I found the most fascinating part of the plane to be the pitot and pitot-static tubes, external sensors that measure velocity. Debris, insects, or ice can sometimes block the pitot tube, which causes airspeed to be measured inaccurately.

If you are a private pilot in a Cessna 182, like I was, a malfunction like this isn't catastrophic. You can still fly visually and manually, using your instinct. However, if these sensors get obstructed on a large commercial aircraft mainly flying on autopilot, catastrophe can result, as it has in a few high-profile disasters.

Like an AI system, the autopilot trusts the veracity or accuracy of its data input and makes decisions based on that fundamental assumption. If the input isn't accurate, wrong decisions are made. For example, Air France 447, traveling between Rio de Janeiro and Paris, crashed into the Atlantic Ocean in 2009. The final report of the BEA, the French agency that investigates airplane accidents, concluded that one or all of the pitot tubes were obstructed by ice crystals, which led to inconsistencies in airspeed measurements. The autopilot ultimately disconnected, and the crew, not knowing what to do with the inconsistent data they were receiving, reacted incorrectly, causing the plane to stall.

Extrapolating, we can see examples of the importance of trusted data inputs to automated systems everywhere. We want our autonomous vehicles to be pulling the correct GPS coordinates as they navigate. What happens if those systems go down or their sensors fail? We want to ensure that medical devices read the correct data and administer the right interventions. Sensors are everywhere.

It's hard to fathom the implications of the proliferation of data that sensors generate. The scale of what can be analyzed runs the gamut from large-scale macro- to very specific micro-behaviors.

One of my first blog posts on this subject was written

after talking with a company that makes a smart electric toothbrush. The data the toothbrush generates—such as whether you are brushing your teeth regularly twice a day—can be shared with third parties like your insurance company or health system. I know this seems ridiculous, which is why I'm sharing it. Even I can't believe it's a true story.

A few years back, I was talking to another insurance carrier on how they could integrate IoT data with their processes. We discussed the smart electric toothbrush example. Besides the question of why in hell someone would want notifications about their toothbrushing, this seems relatively innocuous, right? Wrong. This insurance company was interested in gathering that information and calibrating insurance premiums based on brushing behavior. This is already happening with fitness trackers like the Fitbit and Apple Watch.

This sounded creepy to me. However, as with tracking Oxycontin prescriptions, there may be benefits as well as drawbacks. If you aren't brushing twice a day—thoroughly!—your dental insurance premiums might go up. On the other hand, if you are taking good care of your teeth, your insurance premiums might go down. If there is a problem, your health plan's options can be proactive rather than punitive. You might receive a digital pamphlet on the importance of dental health and could possibly opt in to receive notifications on your cell phone about brushing your teeth right after your alarm gets you up in the morning and just before your usual bedtime.

Taking a broader perspective, insurance companies could create smarter plans optimized by your health behaviors. You could be awarded with lower premiums, for instance, if you went to the gym three times a week.

PRODUCTION AND SHIPPING

The benefits of being able to collect, share, and analyze huge datasets include the optimization of systems and processes. As mentioned in the previous chapter, it may take some time before demand chains become common. Until then, a machine-learning system could optimize inventory for multiple competitive companies based on both overall and regional supply and demand. Companies would be more than willing to participate if such optimization could be shown to be beneficial to all parties—which is probably the case—and would share data as long as the proper blockchain-enabled privacy and security were in place.

Both food production and shipping could be optimized given additional time-specific data on temperature and humidity. The means and speed with which certain agricultural products are shipped could be adjusted in response to real-time conditions. Shipments could take account of data input on local or regional weather, or even market dynamics, such as the interaction between housing prices and the demand for lumber.

The areas in which innovation could occur are endless. Say a shipment involves temperature-controlled drugs. A smart contract stipulates that the shipment needs to stay within certain parameters. If it moves outside them, the goods will be classified as spoiled. If that's the case, the smart contract, based on blockchain-enabled data tracking, would deny release of payment. No one would need to get in the middle. The manufacturer might not like the decision, but it would be uncontroversial, and the manufacturer and shipper would also know they need to pay more attention to temperature changes when transporting the drug in the future.

INTEROPERABILITY

All this depends on blockchain-enabled interoperability. Interoperability is, of course, possible without blockchain. My first company created an API (application program interface) to connect and pull inventory data from the databases of several different clothing companies.

The issue is: does the company that owns and operates one database want to trust the company that owns a second database with all its data? On a broader scale, would fashion brand A and fashion brand B want to enable someone to establish a centralized enterprise that has all the inventory information for every fashion company in the world? This was essentially the result of my first company's initiative.

Of course, I had no nefarious intent for the data. At the time, I simply wanted to provide e-commerce shoppers with a better user experience, one that eliminated annoying affiliate links. That being said, back in 2010, the companies involved were not really privy to the implications of all this. We were just discovering them ourselves. But the business world is far more aware of them now.

Today, interoperability comes down, first, to data privacy. Companies and industries do not want to open up access to data that might reveal competitive business intelligence. Such data privacy is just now becoming possible with blockchain technology's continued development.

The second major requirement and focus are the shared data's validity. With blockchain technology, you know that the data has been collected and shared in a way that ensures privacy. It can't be violated or altered, so the information can be trusted. A distributed blockchain ledger provides a common source of accuracy and validity that third-party data manipulation can't compromise.

Privacy and validity are the two factors that lead to interoperability. That's the real value proposition here. Interoperability is required if multiple datasets are to be accessed, and multiple datasets must be accessed if business-process optimization and similar benefits are to be realized.

PROTOCOLS AND PERMISSIONED BLOCKCHAINS

Blockchain technology can create networks among many different, even competitive, parties based on a common protocol or underlying process. Again, the common protocol underlying the massive network we call the web is http. It's what enables you to access Google, type in a search term, send it back to Google, and receive a list of search results. It also enables you to link to the results in that list, obtaining the information you were looking for in the first place. Of course, we never think about http while doing this.

GS1 for product bar codes is another standard protocol commonly used, but rarely thought about. Visa is another protocol-based network and protocol, and it could also be argued that Google Maps offers a location protocol.

There is, however, no common protocol for sharing the data stored in databases. Quite the contrary. Every company has a different schema or means of identifying and storing data. Data sharing among different databases—company A sharing with company B, B sharing with C, and C sharing with A—still requires messy point-to-point integration.

The data in each of the separate databases needs to be "normalized," given common characteristics, and the datasets must then be mapped onto one another. This is what computer scientists call a nontrivial problem. There are entire companies based on data normalization in every industry. My first company intended to perform this kind of service. Palantir, a Silicon Valley software company co-founded by PayPal co-founder Peter Thiel, is one of the best in the business of data normalization.

A common blockchain-based protocol eliminates the need to normalize data prior to database integration or data sharing. Companies that choose and are permitted to do so can plug into the network—the blockchain—by means of its protocol, adding blocks of their own data and leveraging the data in other blocks provided by other companies. There's no need to have a point-to-point relationship with the other companies on the blockchain network.

This is the almost crazy crux of blockchain. You can exchange data without needing to have any trust in, or even relationship with, your counterparty. Company A doesn't need to have spoken to, or otherwise contacted, companies B, C, D, E, and F to leverage the benefits of their data. In the past, company A would have had to partner with each of the other companies on some level and could then interface with their data only after being allowed to examine their code.

All this implies the development of a number of different protocols, perhaps one for each enterprise blockchain. Http and GS1 standards are meant to be interoperable everywhere and anywhere. If you go to Asia or Europe, you can still get on the web or scan a bar code. A block-chain within a vertical, such as the pharmaceutical industry, requires a separate protocol usable only by those companies that have been given permission to participate.

For this reason, enterprise blockchains will, as I see it, be permissioned based for the time being, as standards are tested and established. It's also why adherents of older, public blockchains, such as bitcoin and Ethereum, don't feel that permissioned blockchains are "real" blockchains.

The genie is already out of the bottle, however. The scalability and privacy benefits of permissioned-based networks are too great not to be pursued. Those bene-fits include increasingly sophisticated machine-learning processing and analysis, which are made possible only by ever-larger datasets. Ultimately, I believe enterprises will move to private data on public networks, but only once standards have been established, the privacy and security of the public networks ensured, and scalability challenges resolved.

OPTIMIZATION IN DAILY LIFE: PRO AND CON

Moving from enterprise to personal applications, let's look at monetary exchanges that take place every day. I recently had a conversation about how often you find yourself without cash and the challenges of tipping under those circumstances. You don't necessarily want to establish the sort of relationship with the person you're tipping that payment systems like PayPal require. Even mobile systems like Venmo require access to a username.

The advantage of bitcoin and other blockchain-based cryptocurrency systems is anonymity. You no longer need to have a trusted relationship with that other party to exchange value. Blockchain allows for interoperability, once again, because you don't need to go through the cumbersome process of point-to-point integration. You don't need to trust or even know your counterparties if they're plugged into a crypto blockchain network.

There is clearly a dystopian dimension to the advanced machine learning that blockchain-based datasets will enable. I sometimes wonder if the world artificial intelligence is creating is one I would want to live in. On the other hand, the trend is undeniable and can't be dealt with by being ignored.

Business trends are market based, and markets as currently constituted rely on continuous growth and increasing efficiency. This leads to optimization through automation, and machine learning or artificial intelligence is a means of automating processes of all kinds. This implies the elimination of inefficiencies, perhaps including human factors. It may not be good, but it's happening, and it's no wonder that shows like *Black Mirror* have become cultural phenomena. I just hope we don't make AI smarter than ourselves.

Moving back to the here and now, let's examine some more specific use cases, starting briefly with "smart" trash collection, which was mentioned in the first chapter, "A Day in the Life Just around the Corner." Again, blockchain will enable all the different trash collection companies and smart trash can manufacturers to interconnect, which will allow trash collectors to plan more efficient routes to keep our cities cleaner and more sustainable.

Of course, this approach has applications in many different industries and contexts, where responses or actions of all types can be triggered by data about whether a certain set of criteria has been met or not. For example, energy grids could be optimized based on data collected by energy usage in areas as large as neighborhoods and city blocks, or as small as houses and apartments—or even individual appliances.

On the dystopian side, many Chinese cities have already put cameras incorporating facial-recognition technology in place. Laws against jaywalking are strongly enforced there, and it is easy to imagine an automated process for collecting data on whether jaywalking has occurred and whether it was you who committed that crime. As mentioned, China has begun to institute a social-credit score. The automated system could then take points off your social-credit score if the data shows you have been jaywalking—or doing any other number of other socially undesirable actions, like walking into the wrong store.

The data interoperability that blockchain enables is beneficial in many respects. Full interoperability could, however, also be used for authoritarian purposes to create the equivalent of a panopticon or surveillance state.

The use case of voting shows the other side of the coin. Smart voting machines could eliminate voter fraud—whether on the part of election boards or voters themselves—and assure accuracy. Blockchain could also make both voter registration and voting itself easier. Mobile voting, enabling a lot more people to cast ballots, would be made possible by blockchain technology's ability to provide absolute verifiability. No more hanging chads! Certain political interests may not want this to happen, but there is no technological reason why such a system couldn't be developed and launched. We could take this a step further and think about blockchain for all governance processes, but we'll save that for the next book!

It's simply a fact that sensorized devices are proliferating, with their size and cost coming down as a function of Moore's law. This will inevitably bring about a growing interest in and fascination with capturing data on as many interactions as possible, with a view to subsequently automating them.

This certainly isn't all bad, in either the political or environmental sphere. Certain countries are net polluters, and some pollute in the extreme. While there are sensors capable of detecting this, the nations involved often tamper with the data these sensors produce. If the data comes straight off the sensor and onto a blockchain, however, it can't be tampered with, and this has positive and possibly global implications.

Moving again to the dystopian side of the spectrum, consider one "great business idea" I heard about and found appalling. Hospitals often lease, rather than own, equipment such as ventilators. An equipment company could, according to the business model that was being pitched, incorporate its lease terms into a smart contract. If those terms weren't met—if, for instance, the hospital failed to meet one or more lease payment—the ventilator would automatically shut down. The originator of this *brilliant* business model didn't seem to take into account—or perhaps didn't care—what would happen to someone on life support if this happened.

Of course, this idea was absolutely and tragically ridiculous, and no one would ever go so far as to implement it. Let's soften this example, however, by applying it to an auto-leasing company: if you don't make a lease payment, the car doesn't turn on.

ETHICAL IMPLICATIONS

There's no shortage of crazy ideas out there inspired by the potential of blockchain technology, but proposed by people who lack the foresight or imagination to see the implications. In 2017, with the proliferation of ICO white papers, there was a great opportunity to see how people come up with often harebrained ideas. It's equally important, in my opinion, to think through the implications of over-automation. AI systems are becoming increasingly powerful, but we need to remember that someone needs to program and train those systems in the first place.

Autonomous or self-driving vehicles, with all the attendant publicity and interest they generate, have become test cases for thinking through ethical and related issues. Say an autonomous vehicle gets into a situation where an accident is inevitable, and the only option is to hit one of several nearby living creatures. The vehicle's AI system would then make a rank-based decision on who would be hit. A pregnant woman or child would be the least likely to be hit. An elderly person might be more likely, a dog even more likely, and a cat the likeliest of all.

What if we put social-credit scores into the mix? For example, the car's AI might decide the jaywalking, alcohol-drinking woman with the marginal social-credit score ranks lower than the bill-paying pregnant one. There are very serious ethical considerations that come into play with advanced technology, which engineers and business-people should diligently consider, but frequently don't.

We're still at a relatively rudimentary stage of blockchain technology and the attendant fourth industrial revolution. Maybe at some point there will be access to enough data that a machine could be trained to be smart enough to make complex judgments. The reality is there are still many unknowns.

For the present and foreseeable future, the human element of making ethical choices remains. I for one don't want to be in a situation in which an automated system, analyzing the data being collected from my ventilator or pacemaker, determines that I have only a short time to live and preemptively decides to take me off life support or shut down my pacemaker remotely.

Some examples, such as energy optimization and pollution control, are clearly improvements, refocusing us on the more positive side of the spectrum. There are other, more ambiguous applications where blockchain technology could create tools that might enable unwanted and unneeded business or government control.

In these cases, the argument that's often advanced is, "Oh, it's just a tool. You can never fully predict or control how someone's going to use it." I think there's more to it than that. It would be gross negligence to develop a system that would be likely to have a negative impact.

On the other hand, there's also a lot of exciting opportunity to improve people's lives. A company that extends credit to individual farmers internationally could use real-time sensor data, combined with historical data on weather and soil conditions, to determine whether it's likely that crops will thrive or fail during the current season.

All this predictive analysis could then enter into a lender's decision-making process. If it's likely to be a bad season, credit could be further extended, possibly at a lower interest rate, enabling farmers to survive the downturn and stay in business. Such data could also be used to boost success rates by, for instance, advising those same farmers when it's time to let a field lie fallow and for how long.

This example has economic and global-trade implications for improving the lives of potentially disenfranchised people at a granular level. The positive implications of optimizing energy and transportation grids through blockchain-enabled data collection and analysis are also both very clear and very exciting. Blockchain has so much potential that it's going to be critical to think through the ethical and other implications involved in implementing this technology.

{ CHAPTER 13 }

RETROFITTING: SECURE COLLABORATION AMONG COMPETITORS

Fragmented supply chains and ecosystems can kill. The smuggling of counterfeit drugs into African and other third-world countries is rampant. In one case, counterfeit malaria pills were sold in Ethiopia. These counterfeits could be detected with a relatively simple lab test: the real pills would dissolve while the counterfeit pills wouldn't. Except that the people relying on the pills to protect them from malaria had no access to the test.

There are so many different players in the pharma industry that things get complicated very quickly. A drug may consist of ten, fifty, or a hundred ingredients obtained from a variety of upstream suppliers. To be certain a medication is what it claims to be, both suppliers and ingredients must be verified.

If the various players in the pharma industry could come together to verify all a drug's components, not only would lives be saved, but greater profits could be made, as business would no longer be lost to illicit trade. It's the classic win-win scenario. Not to mention the uptick in geopolitical stability resulting from eliminating the terrorist and other organizations these markets help fund.

What blockchain-enabled networks are going to make possible in the future is, to a large extent, speculative, but also, given the technology's potential, genuinely exciting. However, blockchain "retrofitting"—applying blockchain technology to increase efficiency and dependability in already established industries—is an equally important application of the technology, especially at this stage. Blockchain is transforming, or poised to transform, some very entrenched verticals.

CASE STUDY: BIG PHARMA

The company I co-founded, Chronicled, has been involved in a major initiative called MediLedger, which links big players in the highly profitable, very competitive pharmaceutical industry. MediLedger uses blockchain to enable these enterprises to collaborate in meeting regulatory standards and drive digital transformation in revenue management and other business processes, while keeping each company's valuable data secure.

This project also serves as a case study for an in-depth, detailed exploration of what can and is being done with blockchain in the enterprise today. What's happening in pharma can help us extrapolate similar applications in other vertical markets. The point is that blockchain, though in an early stage of development, already has very pragmatic uses outside cryptocurrency.

When my co-founders and I formed Chronicled in 2014, the focus was using blockchain technology for the transfer, ownership, and management of physical assets. Blockchain is, above all, a networking tool. Even though, in the early years, individual companies were interested in using blockchain to manage their supply chains, our R & D showed that the technology doesn't really start to unlock value until it is applied to multiparty, rather than individual, networks and transactions.

There must be a driver, a reason for competitive players in an industry to come together to leverage blockchain's benefits by building a multiparty, multisided marketplace. At first glance, it doesn't seem rational that competitors would want to collaborate. This is just not the way business is usually done.

Our experience has been that, much of the time, the core driver bringing competing industry players together in an enterprise network is regulatory compliance. The FDA regulates both food and pharmaceutical safety. Regulations also govern how auto parts and medical devices, among many other products, are tracked.

In 2013, Congress enacted an omnibus pharmaceutical legislation, a major section of which was the Drug Supply Chain Security Act (DSCSA). These FDA-administered regulations, among other things, require that drug manufacturers and distributors—the pharmaceutical industry as a whole—move toward serialization. What this means, first of all, is that every case in a pharmaceutical shipment needs to be uniquely identified.

Why? A wholesaler will often send a drug shipment to a hospital or pharmacy, which might later return it to the wholesaler because they haven't used it or they bought too much. The wholesaler will then resell the drug shipment.

Any time goods change hands in any industry, but particularly in pharmaceuticals, a trust gap opens, first between the manufacturer and distributor, and then between the distributor and retailer or point of sale. The spirit of the regulation was to fight counterfeiting in the pharmaceutical supply chain. Hospitals and pharmacies are where counterfeits will most likely enter the supply chain and it was felt there was not enough oversight at this point in the supply chain.

The first step in this process is assigning pharmaceutical shipments a unique GTIN (global trade identification number) that is GS1 bar code compatible. The second step is a lookup directory able to verify that the drug shipped to the hospital is the same as that which comes back to the wholesaler for resale.

The legislation requires that a fully interoperable system for transferring all this information be in place by 2023. The information will be transferred from a manufacturer, such as Pfizer, to a distributor, such as McKesson, to a dispenser, such as a hospital pharmacy. By that date, all the links in the pharmaceutical supply chain need to be able to share this secure serial-number data and verify it within microseconds. It's almost as if the regulation was written with blockchain in mind, although in 2013, blockchain's applications were still strictly limited to cryptocurrency and unknown except among early adopters.

In response, pharmaceutical companies initially began looking into point-to-point integration of their archaic, twenty-year-old enterprise resource planning (ERP) systems. My first company was involved in this kind of deep systems integration and data normalization, although not in the pharma vertical. If you don't already know, I'll tell you from firsthand experience that this is a huge headache. There was no way that the industry would ever be able to meet DSCSA regulations with the old system, let alone by the 2023 deadline.

Chronicled's MediLedger Project was the first to propose an industry-wide, industry-owned and operated, blockchain-based network to solve the problem. The driver for all this was, once again, regulatory necessity.

There are also consumer drivers for intra-industry cooperation. For example, there are no regulations covering vitamins and supplements, not to mention cosmetics or ethically sourced apparel. However, as mentioned in Chapter 1, consumers want to know that what they're getting is safe and authentic, and that certain product claims can be proven. Are your coffee beans in fact organic, and is the chicken you're about to buy really free range?

It's ironic that regulation is a major driver for enterprise blockchain adoption, since crypto and blockchain were initially proposed as a means of bypassing regulators and similar third parties. Another major shift in what is now going on in industry is a move away from the public nature of the original blockchain networks, where anyone interested could come on board.

While zero-knowledge proofs and other recent advances have been instituted to preserve privacy, most of these weren't part of the original crypto-blockchain infrastructure. Privacy-protecting protocols, however, were essential if blockchain technology was to be brought into the enterprise. Clearly, pharmaceutical companies do not want to share actual serial numbers and other critical inventory data with their competitors. Permissioned-based blockchain technology with built-in privacy has enabled industry competitors to interoperate and use the same resources and tools to meet regulatory requirements, without the fear of competitors and industry analysts accessing the details of the data stored on the directory.

A permissioned pharma blockchain has much wider applicability. Regulation got the players talking, and industry work groups were established to build solutions. What's exciting is the real business value blockchain can generate. Blockchains are interoperable multiparty networks, but don't need to be industry-wide. They can be built for consortiums within an industry, span verticals, and even manage complex vendor networks for large multinational corporations. In short, they can unlock value by instituting entirely new business models and ways of doing business.

Pharmaceutical contracting and revenue management is

very complicated and involves lengthy, messy cycles. A manufacturer might offer a rebate to a dispenser on the other end of the supply chain, but the wholesaler sitting in the middle often has a different deal—all involving cumbersome rebates and chargebacks.

The resulting complicated three-party financial transactions are all handled manually at this point. There are entire floors of people dedicated to the manual reconciliation of chargebacks in the pharma industry. There's no specific data on what this costs the industry, but, if I had to guess, I'd speculate it to be in the millions or even hundreds of millions per year.

To make matters even more complicated, pharma mergers and the acquisition of licenses for drug IP are very common, occurring far more frequently than you might imagine. All this makes it difficult to automate relationship maintenance.

This process became the next use case, after adherence to DSCSA regulations, for the MediLedger network. By automating chargebacks, the industry could unlock millions of dollars of value annually. That got everyone excited. Businesses want to be efficient and to save as well as make money.

The original regulatory driver brought together companies in a traditionally slow-moving industry. In the beginning, the pharma companies didn't know what blockchain was and put up resistance: "This is smoke-and-mirrors technology." After having seen the power of solutions that can automate complex transactions in the snap of a finger, they got enthusiastically on board. Pharma companies now get excited when they see demos of what's possible.

BUILDING ECOSYSTEMS

Of course, none of this happens overnight, nor does it happen according to a preestablished playbook. Instead, working groups were established to gather requirements and prioritize needs throughout the industry. One of the critical elements of these working groups was social.

Few people realize that social engineering or community and ecosystem building is, by far, the most critical element in building blockchain networks. Blockchain is a powerful technology, but it's much more than a technology. It supports and enables shifts in the social paradigm that began before the technology was built or even proposed. Blockchain and crypto are results and symptoms of changing cultural needs, a movement toward decentralization, interoperability, and automation.

Community is a process, and there's a face-to-face,

human element at work in blockchain. People are social animals. They set up work groups, wine and dine, and arrange conferences. Whatever the social element might be, once you get people in a room—physical or virtual—they can start innovating. If one company moves forward, the others know they need to do likewise to remain competitive. Now they realize that in some respects they can do so together.

PRIVATE "BLOCKCHAINS"

It's still too early to say where we're at and what aspects of today's approaches will persist. However, it's instructive to compare an analogous, but different approach in another industry. Maersk, the shipping giant, partnered with IBM to go to market with a shipping-consortium blockchain. It's hard to say what their approach was or whether they established a working group or fostered interpersonal relationships during the two years of development prior to launch. However, since launch, they've had a hard time getting other companies involved.

Maersk is the second-biggest shipping company in the world, and it wouldn't be surprising if other industry players were highly suspicious of their blockchain initiative: "We're not stupid. We're not going to join together to support and add value to this huge, competitive shipping company that's overhauling the network." There's a far more complex social dynamic at work here as well: the need to preserve sufficient decentralization and proper governance in any blockchain network.

Look at crypto blockchains operating under a proof of work or even proof-of-stake basis. They are and must be sufficiently decentralized to prevent an attack by 51 percent of the community. The whole point of blockchain is its immutability. Because the network is decentralized, it can't be taken over and its records can't be changed.

It's not entirely clear whether private or even permissioned networks are adequately decentralized. It's more likely that this is the case in a permissioned blockchain like the one my company built for the pharmaceutical industry, where many different manufacturers and service providers are running nodes. However, what would happen if one of these partners amassed 51 percent or more of the network's resources?

The limitations of fully private blockchains are much clearer, in my opinion. IBM has developed a blockchain for Maersk that Maersk controls. This is not to say that the blockchain could not evolve and achieve sufficient decentralization by inviting more companies to be blockchain nodes or members and part of its governance.

However, as things stand, in this example the blockchain

could hardly be called decentralized. Any other shipping firm that might join the network would be unable to do so as a genuine peer, so they don't join. Similarly, Walmart is now getting into the pharmaceutical industry, but no one else in the industry is going to want to work with a Walmart blockchain, since Walmart's MO is to establish hegemony, taking over as much as they can as fast as they can.

What we're seeing now is industries in which super powerful players are going up against even more powerful ones. So crypto and, by extension, blockchain maximalists may well have a point. Public networks are where the real innovation—both in terms of technology and business models—is going to take place. What's critical are security, privacy, and decentralization.

The pharma blockchain working groups were able to come together more quickly than anticipated. Much of this was due to team effort and persistence in both building community and identifying concrete solutions involving a clear return on investment. This wasn't just an R&D project where infrastructure was being developed for infrastructure's sake. The blockchain infrastructure that was developed solves a real problem and saves costs. A lot of current blockchain projects aren't doing that yet.

COUNTERFEIT AND DIVERTED GOODS

Retrofitted, blockchain-enabled, supply-chain applications could address problems that trust gaps have caused in many industries. Lack of collaboration leads to such gaps opening up between almost every company, database, and exchange in a vertical market. Counterfeit goods are a major problem across many industries. This affects not only pharmaceuticals, but the food we eat; cosmetics and personal care products, such as shampoo; and auto parts, such as airbags. You name it. A large percentage of counterfeit components have even been found in Air Force One! Counterfeit circuit boards and radios are found in many US Air Force jets.

A lot of focus has been put on counterfeit luxury goods, but this problem is sometimes seen as relatively trivial in the larger scheme of things. If the argument is made that counterfeit goods are cutting away at a luxury company's sales, the company will probably reply, "No, they're not. The people who want to and can buy a Louis Vuitton handbag will go to the store and buy it. It's the people who can't afford one who buy the fakes. In fact, this makes our products more desirable and builds brand value."

In the case of luxury goods, it's almost like the industry doesn't want to solve the counterfeiting problem. As odd and counterintuitive as this is, luxury brands think of counterfeiting as adding brand value, even though no one will actually go so far as to admit believing this.

When products are applied to the body, like cosmetics, or ingested, like food, pharmaceuticals, vitamins, and supplements, the risks become clearer. However, cosmetic companies, when asked if counterfeiting and diversion are creating difficulties, will still sometimes respond, "We wish we had that problem. That would mean our brand has the consumer awareness we want to build."

It's clearly very serious if a counterfeit airbag blows up in people's faces and kills them. At one point, I was in an Uber and the driver had one of those fake iPhone chargers you can buy for a dollar. It burst into flames while we were driving, and it's fortunate nothing worse happened. On a larger scale, counterfeit goods clearly contribute to illicit trade markets, which, in turn, fuel geopolitical instability and terrorism, among other global problems.

Everyone's been touched by counterfeits, whether they know it or not. I think the big challenge here is that people generally don't know if they're buying a counterfeit. Perhaps ignorance is bliss, although I doubt it. I do know that the penetration of counterfeited goods into the consumer market can't help but make me paranoid about what I'm buying.

Diversion is an overlapping problem. Diverted products are sold through channels the original vendor or brand hasn't authorized, and such products are often subject to tampering.

Amazon, because it is a free-for-all marketplace, is a major venue for the sale of counterfeit or diverted goods. Amazon, of course, doesn't encourage this. Quite the contrary. However, if you're buying Yeezy sneakers on Amazon, you can be fairly sure they are fake.

Why hasn't this issue, which affects almost every industry, been addressed more fully? Once the need is acknowledged, blockchain technology has the potential to solve the problem, given the necessary focus and resolve. For instance, a consortium of companies in an industry such as personal care and cosmetics or vitamins and supplements could join together to build a blockchain to verify and certify products without giving away competitive data.

BLOCKCHAIN VERIFICATION

Consumers, more than regulation, are the real drivers here. People generally trust Whole Foods, for instance, which Amazon has now acquired. The price of avocados has suddenly gone from $4 to $1.99 apiece, which seems great, but are the avocados now on sale still being grown organically and sustainably?

It comes down to the question of whether consumers can trust the food they eat and products they consume. What about baby food and household cleaners? What if, like Alice in Chapter 1, you insist on fair-trade coffee? What if you have celiac disease and really do need everything you eat to be gluten-free?

Most goods and products arrive in our homes at the end of complex globalized supply chains, meaning that trust gaps continue to get wider. Industries and consumers need to come together to form communities and rebuild trust through verifiability.

Blockchain technology is, among other things, a verification tool, a distributed, unalterable, time-stamped ledger capable of proving an event occurred. A blockchain can substantiate that the coffee beans in your kitchen were picked at such a place at such a time under specific—organic, fair-trade—conditions, and then were shipped by a specific company to a specific point of sale.

There are areas where it's nice to know a product is authentic and others where it's critical. Both cases are important. There are also considerable financial implications for art collectors, wine collectors, and the trade in diamonds and other gems. The value of any such investment or asset ultimately depends on authentication.

A MATTER OF LIFE OR DEATH

Still more serious are forensic-evidence, chain-of-custody issues. Maintaining chain of custody is crucial to our legal system. A broken chain of custody puts evidence, and the results of any ruling or trial verdict made on the basis of that evidence, into question. The problem lies on both sides of the scale: A mistrial can be declared if a chain of evidence is broken, even though the verdict was accurate. On the other hand, people have gone to jail who shouldn't have because a chain of custody was mistakenly or falsely verified.

Prison or freedom and life or death. Although I'm a pilot and a skydiver, I don't really like flying. Say a screw is counterfeit or a genuine part hasn't been properly tested. Little things, like a broken nut or weak threads on a bolt, are capable of causing big disasters. The same is true of medical devices.

In short, there are any number of instances in which verifiability has either financial or life-and-death implications, where blockchain technology can and will prove itself useful. My prediction is that the closer that a product gets to the body, the earlier and more likely the companies manufacturing it will be to adopt blockchain.

The same is true of environmental issues. Denim is the second-biggest water polluter in the world. The industry is aware of this problem and its environmental impact. Competing companies in the vertical are talking about blockchain solutions to measure and reduce pollution by keeping each other accountable.

BUILDING THE ECOSYSTEM

Is this actually going to happen or is it pie in the sky? Consumers say they care if their clothing is ethically and sustainably sourced. But when it comes to buying decisions, it's unclear whether enough consumers are really concerned enough to pay a premium. At the very least, there is now a technology that can unalterably verify product claims.

A lot of industries are exploring blockchain for just this reason. However, once again, what really needs to come first is community. Before you can spin up a blockchain, a group needs to come together in a specific marketplace to discuss the need for, and applications of, the technology.

The challenge to building enterprise blockchains in the consumer space is the absence of marketplace liquidity early in a product's development-and-distribution process. This is a variation on the classic chicken-or-egg dilemma. Even a double-sided marketplace like eBay needs to attract both inventory and buyers. Which comes first?

Blockchain has the capacity to build out still more complex marketplaces consisting of multiparty transactions and interactions. That's its real strength. But multiparty, blockchain-based marketplaces are not easy to build, in terms of either infrastructure or the ecosystems to support them.

Ecosystem building is the most critical, yet underrated and undervalued, aspect of blockchain development. Consumers have now grown up in a user-friendly era, with the expectation that they can quickly log in to apps that are going to run quickly and smoothly.

In exchange for these conveniences, we've sold ourselves and our data. We're now starting over again, with Web 2.0's benefits and drawbacks clearly in mind. We want decentralization, self-sovereign identity, and true data ownership. However, the user experience for most blockchain networks is still really clunky. While a lot of people maintain that a seamless, well-designed user experience has to come first, a conversation about pros, cons, and alternatives is at least starting to happen.

What tends to be overlooked is that the fundamental reason user experience needs to be "seamless" is because it's what attracts an ecosystem or community. Typically, when a tech product is developed, it's developed for a persona, the representative of a target demographic.

Members of this demographic share the same pain point or problem, which the product will solve.

When building a blockchain-based decentralized app (dApp), you'll probably be dealing with three or more different personas, if that term is used to imply the different needs, expectations, and roles in a complex interaction. A good analogy to such business processes is a biological ecosystem built of any number of different interacting elements.

What's needed is marketing in the broadest sense of the word: making a case that will bring people together. Marketing tends to be underestimated among crypto and blockchain fundamentalists. However, I'd say that Satoshi and the people behind bitcoin were fantastic marketers. First and foremost, they were able to launch a technology in the service of a social movement, almost a religion, in a very strategic fashion.

A lot of people in the blockchain industry—if it can even be called that yet—are technologists or developers first. They believe that the critical issue is building out infra-structure and theirs is the most important role in making the technology viable.

Of course the developer role is critical. But the most critical? I'm helping out a friend who is managing PR for the Decred cryptocurrency. Decred is an ecosystem of thousands of people who all vote and participate in open, real-time communications on forums and Slack channels. This is beyond being a multisided marketplace. It's a completely decentralized ecosystem. The technology only means something if people actually use it, and that's what intelligent marketing and public relations can help make happen.

Web 2.0 is dead, or so investors are beginning to believe. We've discovered that the massive social-network platforms that everyone and anyone can get on are invitations to massive data breaches. What's emerging instead are smaller-scale ecosystems or niche communities. Things are going back to the days of Web 1.0, where there were chat rooms and other specific communities of interest. But with a difference—a different technology and a different perspective.

We're moving on to Web 3.0.

CHAPTER 14

BUILDING A BLOCKCHAIN-BASED CULTURE

Web 2.0 is great. Or, at least, it enables me to do a lot of things I couldn't do otherwise. I can buy my airline tickets five minutes before getting on a plane, jump in an Uber, and order my food on Instacart. Very convenient.

TaskRabbit is another Web 2.0 service I find very useful: a marketplace that helps you find and contact local handypeople when you need help assembling furniture or hanging things on your walls. One day, what I needed was someone to hang a television monitor on the wall of my new apartment in New York.

After booking through TaskRabbit, I got an email from them. I'm generally very careful to check return addresses to avoid phishing schemes. This email came from an address at taskrabbit.com, so I opened it. I clicked a "confirm" link in the email, which then brought me to a weird code-hosting site. Suddenly the screen on the site melted away and I got one of those "Ha, ha, got you!" messages.

I was then taken to a website revealing confidential Task-Rabbit revenue and employee information, which then also disappeared. As a tech-security type, I took screen-shots of the whole process and posted them on my Twitter account, tagging TaskRabbit, asking them if they knew they were undergoing a security breach. It was all very weird. I was seeing a hack in real time!

Although I didn't get a direct reply from TaskRabbit, my screenshots were re-tweeted and started appearing elsewhere on the web. It eventually came out that there had in fact been a breach. TaskRabbit sent the standard email to everyone in their marketplace: "We've had a security breach. The site will be down for a while. Change all your passwords, not just on our website, but every website you've ever used. If you logged in through Facebook, you'll have to change all your Facebook-related passwords."

I had in fact signed in with Facebook, which compounded the hassle. I probably still haven't gotten around to changing all the relevant passwords. The system is so complicated, with so many passwords, that you don't even know what you're logged into anymore.

In other words, we've got a problem: Web 2.0.

The solution, Web 3.0, will revisit the sociocultural principles and ideals behind Web 1.0 in the context of a whole new technology. Web 3.0 is poised to solve the problems of Web 2.0, but this is going to demand time, work, and patience.

THE WEB 2.0 DILEMMA

Web 2.0 basically just blew up. Its social networks have now become massive, consolidated, and eminently hackable.

There's been a Facebook hack, an Equifax hack, and, in late November 2018, a hack of the Marriott website, in which data on five-hundred-million of their guests was compromised. It's started to feel like some massive data breach occurs a couple times every week. Even the US government runs on G Suite products, which is just crazy, given all the user data this allows Google to collect.

Both Facebook and Google have now been the targets of Congressional investigations. The biggest concern, of course, is over Facebook's collusion—certainly passive and possibly active—in elections here and abroad, notably the US presidential election in 2016. Mark Zuckerberg has testified before Congress and was also called before the British Parliament. He didn't show up to give testimony, so he may be in considerable trouble in the UK.

When all the news about possible voter manipulation started coming out, a lot of people suddenly woke up, realizing that centralization on this level is quite dangerous. Facebook is bigger than any individual country in terms of population, although China gives it a run for its money. This means its control is now being exerted on a global level.

This isn't a conspiracy in the sense that Facebook set out to become a cabal. It's all been hidden in plain sight. The effects are devastating, nevertheless. It's all the outcome of the unbridled growth and monopolistic tendencies of Web 2.0 companies like Google and Facebook. Web 2.0 technology made harvesting massive amounts of user data possible, and what was possible soon became inevitable.

Global networks can influence elections in Africa and South America simultaneously. They impact international trade and other relationships. Global connectivity and interoperability aren't the problem. In fact, they're a benefit. The problem is having just a few companies in control of everything that's going on, and all this has happened very quickly.

The ease of communication and access to knowledge

that Web 2.0 has provided helps everyone. However, there's also a darker side. The issue is one of restoring privacy and security—reestablishing trust—while maintaining connectivity. Then there are the constraints that systems like Facebook and Gmail place on users. Most people aren't aware of these, but they have negative consequences just the same. My Google Docs files are all traceable and searchable. Perhaps not by the public at large, but by Google and hackers able to breach the system. The same goes for Dropbox.

WEB 3.0 SOLUTIONS

The underlying ethos of what we now call Web 3.0 is, in contrast, truly peer-to-peer. What does a peer-to-peer network mean for users? It makes them more autonomous, powerful, and independent. It protects their privacy, is secure, and gives them control over their own identities and data.

A good example of the new paradigm is how the future of work is changing: from having a single employer, first to the gig economy, and then to sovereign individuals who contribute to one or many projects on their own initiative. These values are rooted in the open-source software movement: autonomous community members constantly changing and improving a system open to their input. Its organizational culture is flat—peer-to-peer—a holarchy rather than a hierarchy.

You participate by just jumping in and connecting on Slack, Discord, WhatsApp, Signal, or one of the many other communications tools that have enabled the creation of distributed teams. If you have an idea for a project, you just submit it, and community members vote on whether they will support it. If they vote yes, you submit a contractor invoice detailing the time you put in on the project, and community members vote on whether to approve the invoice.

This is clearly not a typical business organizational structure. However, it does coincide in critical ways with what's going on in the workforce at large. The future of work is distributed and remote, not centralized. A large percentage of the US workforce is already made up of members of the gig economy.

There will be a whole new range of tools to support this cultural shift, including improved video conference platforms and augmented reality (AR) and virtual reality (VR). Secure communications channels are critical in this context. The data being transmitted needs to be protected, trusted, and self-sovereign. Proprietary work conversations can't be broadcast through the Facebook distribution machine.

What I envision for Web 3.0 is networks of independent, autonomous community members—rather than "users"—

participating because they enthusiastically choose to, rather than because they are required to. We will see if this actually happens, because these ideas were around at the dawn of the internet and, to date, things haven't played out the way they were originally envisioned.

RE-EXAMINING THE WEB 1.0 ERA

It's helpful to go back to the future and take a look at Web 1.0's strengths and values. While 1994 was the year the first truly usable web browser, Netscape Navigator, was launched, 1999 was the year that Napster, the controversial file-sharing service, appeared.

In a sense, Napster was "very Web 3.0," in that is was fundamentally peer-to-peer. I used Napster to download music when I was a kid. All of a sudden, the government cracked down on sharing music files, a practice the recording industry branded piracy. My parents told me to stop downloading music, because the cops would come arrest me if I didn't. In fact, a couple of arrests were made—seemingly as warnings—and Napster ceased to operate as a file-sharing service.

Spotify and similar Web 2.0 services have now made streaming music available to everyone. The problem—solvable with blockchain technology—is that the service pays very little or nothing to the musicians who created the music. Yes, it's a complex ecosystem, but the question remains: who's the pirate now?

The same holds for communications. When Web 1.0 came along, it was quite novel to be able to send an email message across the world in an instant without using a fax machine. Chat rooms opened up, and all this became a new way of accessing information, making human connections, and driving globalization.

People, of course, still use email. As Web 2.0 has evolved, a number of other special-use communication systems and networks have arisen, including flagship social networks like Facebook. Originally solutions to the problem of one-to-many communication, these have now become part of the problem.

A paradigm or philosophical shift is now taking place where everything old is new again, except that Web 3.0 networks have the potential to be much better—far more usable—than Web 1.0 communication systems were. Members of the tech and crypto communities are now spending more and more of their time on blockchain-enabled platforms, which are both more democratic and more secure than the Web 2.0 megaliths. These are platforms where you own your own identity, data, and tools.

Web 3.0 has the potential to become a system of interlocking, but self-sovereign networks you can log on to with a single identity you yourself own, as opposed to putting your information and login credentials onto every website. It's a great solution to my TaskRabbit-hack problem.

THE SHIFT FROM WEB 2.0 TO WEB 3.0

People have been writing about and fighting for this new paradigm all along. However, changing global systems is a complex process. Cryptocurrency set itself up in contrast to the globalized financial system. Demand chains are fundamentally different from supply chains. Blockchain-enabled communications channels will be built on technology much different than that underlying Web 2.0 social networks.

We'll see shifts in major players across all categories from file storage to banking, media, supply chains, governance and government, and how we conceive of what work is in the first place. Companies that are the current behemoth leaders, like Uber, Dropbox, and even Amazon, may be displaced and will certainly need to evolve.

The current paradigm is deeply entrenched, however. It's being challenged, but we're still in such an early stage that it's doubtful we can yet fully fathom what will emerge. Both Facebook and Amazon are investing in building out their blockchain resources, so we'll have to see how this all plays out.

In the current phase, Web 3.0 projects still look at existing networks and try to replicate and decentralize them at the same time. I think this just shows that we're still in a very early stage of the transformation.

Take Uber, a centralized Web 2.0-based network, as an example. What Web 3.0 makes possible is a decentralized Uber: a network that does what Uber does—gets you a ride from point A to point B—but which is owned and operated not by a centralized company, but by the drivers and other people who work there, as well as by the riders themselves.

The drivers remain freelancers, but get paid better wages with benefits, an improvement made possible because there is no centralized "Uber" company taking its commission or cut. Drivers and riders will be full stakeholders in this "Web 3.0 Uber" network, able to participate in the decisions that impact them, their work, and the service.

This shift's potential to change behavior and community formation is ideological and perhaps even political in nature. Again, it's yet to be seen how this will play out. However, what's going to happen will not be just a repeat performance: "Let's build a new Amazon, but a decentralized one." Something more powerful is about to happen that will unlock new business models and modes of interaction. It will be exponentially transformative, an evolution of thought, connection, and community.[1]

BUSINESS MODELS TRANSFORMED

Globally connected groups of autonomous and independent participants whose alignment is based on incentives they themselves determine and freely choose? The vision is utopian, and entrenched interests are not going to give up without a fight. The possibility of co-opting blockchain technology to perpetuate and further entrench current systems is very real.

While I think that permissioned enterprise blockchains have tremendous potential, I do find the notion of using the technology to support existing systems, as opposed to helping define new ones, problematic. I'm confident, however, that retrofitting might turn out to be something like putting training wheels on a bike. When we finally take them off, and financial, enterprise, and other blockchain systems are in place, we'll be operating in a whole new world with business models we could never before imagine.

---

1   I hate buzzwords. I particularly detest the word "disrupt." No one wants to be disrupted, so why say it? Evolution is far more elegant and accurate.

Crypto may have begun with the gamers, hackers, and developers hidden behind the curtains and Twitter pseudonyms. Satoshi Nakamoto's white paper, however, was consciously positioned in opposition to the global financial system, proposing units of value outside the bounds of the money created and endorsed by government fiat. Now, institutional investors are involved in crypto, perhaps either because of an "if you can't beat 'em, join 'em" impulse or with a FOMO (fear of missing out) desire to profit by getting in early.

Pro or con, all these developments show the power and potential of blockchain technology. Is co-optation inevitable? As of 2019, there were Facebook postings for blockchain engineers, leading to speculation that the WhatsApp chat messaging app Facebook acquired may soon be blockchain based. Perhaps this is meant to facilitate crypto payments on a global level and help position WhatsApp to compete with China's WeChat. Amazon and Bank of America are making similar hires. It seems like all these huge companies now have blockchain initiatives. Alibaba, the Chinese Amazon, has the most blockchain patents in the world.

Co-opting blockchain technology may help Web 2.0 companies go through a business transformation. However, in my opinion, there's no way in the world that the Facebook we know today can or ever will decentralize.

Decentralization is, however, critical to the realization of the real potential of the blockchain-based Web 3.0 infrastructure as its build-out continues. Web 3.0 won't meet past expectations, but will differ from and surpass them, creating ways of interacting that weren't previously possible.

WHERE ARE WE HEADED?

Gaming trends often give a glimpse of the future, so let's take a look. Esports are now bigger than the NFL. However, most people watching esports remain spectators, just as they do when watching conventional media like television and the movies. Online, we're still by and large passive consumers of data, information, and entertainment, as opposed to more active participants in our own lives. We're also mindless producers, creating content that ultimately supports the social platform we're using more than it supports us.

Web 3.0 and blockchain, on the other hand, enable active transactions of all kinds. Let's look at a small, but significant shift. Gamers have taken to streaming other players' *Fortnite* games on Twitch. Since blockchain technology facilitates micropayments, these spectators occasionally send tips to the players they're watching in the form of tokens. This changes the way the game is played, turning spectators into participants. Similarly, a viewer acquiring and sending a player an in-game sword can change the outcome of a battle.

Dark Mirror's "Bandersnatch" episode on Netflix was an experiment in interactive storytelling, a video version of the Choose Your Own Adventure books. The next step might be to enable small crypto exchanges that would impact storylines, opening up new ways of interacting with media, as well as new content business and revenue models. Distributed systems enable a paradigm shift from passive consumption to active participation.

Moving from gaming to the world of work: what will further enabling people from all over the world to communicate and collaborate on projects mean? Joe Lubin's Ethereum-based company ConsenSys got some bad press when the crypto market fell in late 2018. However, the company has to be given credit for experimenting with holocracy and a system where employees distributed all over the world can jump on and off projects at will or as needed. The company clearly needed more of an operational and structural focus, but the two impulses can and should complement one another, rather than cancel each other out.

On a larger scale, will people continue flocking to cities, intensifying urbanization, or will they become more geographically distributed as our companies and businesses become less centralized? I've worked on a project with people in Thailand, Berlin, San Francisco, and Ukraine. I've also worked with people living in the same city I was.

The first industrial revolution led to increasing urbanization, as workers migrated into cities to be near factory jobs. Going back much further in time, the agricultural revolution led to people who had previously been nomadic hunter-gatherers settling down in villages. What's taking place now in the fourth industrial revolution may be as significant in terms of scale.

Seemingly insignificant incidents are often symbolic of profound shifts. Crypto started with a white paper and the movement proliferated with a developer buying a couple of Pizzas with bitcoin. "Bitcoin Pizza" seems whimsical, but when all is said and done, it's no joke. Buying those Pizzas may or may not have been the first crypto transaction ever—in fact, it almost certainly wasn't—but it's the first that's been immortalized in an origin story that's now remembered and retold. Similarly, the spinning jenny, invented in 1764, though a small machine with a relatively trivial application, pointed the way to the first industrial revolution.

In the same way, people a hundred or two hundred years from now may look back at the period we're now entering and see it as a time where the fabric of human society shifted. When I was in grad school, I argued in my master's thesis that global, multinational corporations and social-media networks had transcended national boundaries and gone a level up. What happens now if we go a level beyond that? Decentralized blockchain networks may lead to people creating their own independent sources of revenue, interacting peer-to-peer in the smallest to largest of contexts.

What then happens to the current global financial system? Will people be accumulating and storing? Will they be investing, and what will they be investing in? We now invest in gold, artwork, wine, and property. We invest in markets through mutual funds and 401(k) pension plans. Some people want "safe jobs" where their employers will match their 401(k) contributions. Crypto fundamentalists, in contrast, smirk at all this, believing conventional markets are on the way out.

While global financial collapse of this kind is unlikely, it's safe to assume we'll be living in an increasingly digital or digitally mediated world. Walk outside and you'll see half the people coming down the street with their faces in their phones—unless they've got Apple AirPods stuck in their ears. I'm plugged into my computer so much of the day that I sometimes feel I'm half robot.[2] It seems like a

2   If you'd seen my "pulse: 0" readings on Apple Watches and exercise equipment, you'd probably think I was one. In fact, my trainer is convinced I am!

lot of us are bionic now, and this is even truer of Gen Z digital natives. They've bypassed Facebook because it's their parents' network.

It's simply true that we're now living simultaneously in the real and digital worlds. "Real" or physical transactions are appropriate in the former and digital transactions in the latter. Many of us are spending half our time in the digital realm already, and it makes complete sense that our transactions in that realm will involve digital assets. One reason gaming is so important is because this has been and is happening there first.

Blockchain technology has the potential to provide the infrastructure for transformative cultural shifts that now seem like science fiction. Joe Lubin's ConsenSys acquired Planetary Resources, the asteroid mining company, in October 2018. Ethereum has positioned itself as a global supercomputer generating hundreds or thousands of different decentralized blockchain protocols to enable a gamut of transactions and exchanges.

While we're on the topic of space travel, let's talk about Elon Musk. He founded SolarCity, which later merged with Tesla. Many think that company's objective is to build cars. Sure, they're building cars for consumers here on Earth, but what they're really doing is innovating on batteries and energy storage.

Batteries? Check.

Then there is the Boring Company, which is building the Hyperloop, a glorified fast-moving subway system in LA. Is it really building a subway system or is it advancing tunneling technology?

Tunneling tech? Check.

And we have NeuraLink, which is quite literally working to upload human consciousness into a machine.

Humanoid robots? Check.

We have OpenAI, which is advancing AI systems.

AI? Check.

And finally, we have SpaceX, which is sending rockets out into space and plans to colonize Mars.

Mars colony? Check.

All told, what we have is an ecosystem working to upload human consciousness into robots, advance them with AI, establish a Mars colony, and power these machines, the robots and tunnel diggers, with advanced-battery energy-storage systems. And you thought that humans would be the ones to settle the Red Planet? Think again.

But let's come back down to Earth.

Does the not-so-distant future look like *WALL-E*, where the people are so plugged in that they pay no attention to their bodies or physical surroundings? Does it look like *The Matrix*, where people are literally linked to machines that run on the energy they generate? Will those energy-intensive machines be mining bitcoin?

Let's hope not! While it seems inevitable that we will be increasingly more connected with the digital and less connected with the physical realm, this will, or so I hope, drive more value and meaning back to the "real world."

We have to maintain our humanity. I hope we don't get so connected to and reliant on blockchain-based networks and other emerging technologies that we lose the under-lying human element in our transactions. Sometimes I actually just want to run down to the corner store and have a brief exchange with another person.

We've already begun to move away from owning homes, cars, and other assets. What does this say about the values and aspirations of the coming generation? My sense is that truly decentralized peer-to-peer networks open completely new possibilities for human autonomy and connection. My hope is that we will use the technology to restore connections with ourselves, our communities, our environment, and what we consume. Only then will we begin to heal the trust that has been so deeply wounded over the past century.

CONCLUSION

Yes, calling this book *Bitcoin Pizza* was a bit facetious. But, hey, I just really love Pizza. I can't help it if it also was a great way of getting your attention. So, hell, if I'm going to spend all the time it takes to write a book, I'd better like what I'm doing.

The title also had a serious purpose. Origin stories are culturally important. Myths and collective mythmaking are how we create the narratives that shape collective consciousness. There's the book of Genesis, George Washington and the cherry tree, and Steves Jobs and Wozniak starting Apple in a garage.

I've spent some time traveling and conducting anthropology research on origin stories and collective mythmaking in the context of both nation-states and corporations. You can't help but notice that, in every community, the role of myth and, more specifically, the origin story shapes not only culture and values, but, more broadly, reality.

Examples of the role of origin stories with cohesive narratives in establishing culture and society could be multiplied indefinitely. Bitcoin Pizza is crypto and blockchain's.

The mysterious, pseudonymous Satoshi Nakamoto and his 2008 white paper are a critical part of this narrative, which touches on such fundamental social issues as the way people interact, do business, and exchange data and information. Was Satoshi an individual, a small cadre of people, or a group ten thousand strong? Was Satoshi the pseudonymous artist Banksy? Is Banksy the front man for the band Massive Attack? An entire book on the power of pseudonymous characters in shaping history could be written. Everyone loves a good mystery.

Timing is also critical in storytelling, and the bitcoin white paper strategically appeared just at the moment people felt most burned by the global financial system and were therefore most receptive to alternatives. There had, in fact, been ten white papers about the technology released in the previous decade, one by Nick Szabo, one of the primary candidates for the man behind Satoshi. Satoshi's paper was the one that hit the bull's-eye.

When Satoshi's manifesto appeared, most people had

already taken the step of supplying Web 2.0 websites with their identities: their real names, credit card numbers, bank information, and so on. That hadn't been true in the early Web 1.0 days, when people were still using avatars and screen names. By 2008, and increasingly in more recent years, the data submitted has been hacked, misused, or otherwise compromised.

Bitcoin Pizza was not the first crypto transaction on the bitcoin network. There had certainly been earlier tests. But the story of a multimillion-dollar Pizza has a humorous, down-home appeal, and it's what gets remembered. The amount of money involved—and especially the astronomical increase in value involved—really caught people's attention.

A lot of these kinds of transactions took place between 2009 and 2017, some of them involving gamers and gaming, and some on the dark web. It was in 2017, however, that the mass media really started becoming interested in bitcoin, crypto, and blockchain, and the enormous increase in what had been paid for bitcoin Pizza was a vivid and convenient hook for its stories.

Once crypto went mainstream, due to the tremendous spike in bitcoin valuation, misunderstanding and misinterpretation inevitably arose. Crypto came to be seen not as a decentralized means of exchange, but a speculative asset. The craze for tokens, altcoins, and what ultimately turned out to be sh*tcoins took off. There was an over-abundance of ICOs, some of which were quite sketchy. Institutional investors suddenly got interested.

Amidst the feeding frenzy, most people were unaware of the cyclical nature of the crypto market: the bull and bear markets, booms and busts, that had already occurred and were bound to reoccur. This book is subtitled *The No-Bullshit Guide to Blockchain* because there's been so much misunderstanding about what blockchain and crypto are and do, and I'm here to give it to you straight: no bullshit.

Mythology is powerful, and origin stories are perhaps the most powerful myths of all. We're still at the beginning of the Web 3.0 revolution, and what interests me most about blockchain is the role it's poised and is already beginning to play in the sociocultural shift to decentralization.

The influence of technology on culture has been critical ever since the first paleolithic stone knives. Farming was the technology behind the agricultural revolution, which many biologists believe had an effect on the evolution of the human brain. The first wave of industrialization led away from purely local production—the local cobbler or tailor—to greater geographical dispersion. Once Ford introduced his production line, not only did all his competitors have to follow suit or get sucked under, but the horse and buggy was replaced by the automobile, which practically defines the world we now live in. All these technologies created massive social and cultural shifts.

When we think of technology today, we tend to focus on computing, software, and the web. These technologies have already caused enormous changes in the way we interact and do business. It wasn't that long ago that it was considered crazy to go overseas and develop a relationship with a Chinese company to manufacture products to be sold back here in the States. If you wanted to do something like that, you had to get on a plane to meet with the people involved, as Steve Jobs had to do when he wanted to enlist Japanese designers to work with Apple.

Such arrangements are no longer rare or unusual. In fact, they're commonplace. As the web developed and computing power continued to increase exponentially, as Moore's law predicted, global financial networks arose, as did automated trading, derivatives, and many other complex financial products. Increased connectivity saw the development of ever more complicated global supply chains: a product is manufactured in one country, packaged in another, and sent to a distribution center here in the States. We order it on Amazon, and a drone drops it off at our house.

There are cons as well as pros to all this, and these include, but aren't limited to, the 2008 financial crisis. Globalization has brought about a sense of disconnection. A countertrend has developed, pulling back from globalization and leading to political fallout such as Brexit. Web 2.0 technology has amplified this sense of alienation, with people increasingly addicted to social platforms purpose-built to keep them clicking and supplying harvestable data. What is supposed to be connecting us—the web—seems to be doing the opposite.

The resulting disillusionment and distrust have created an environment ripe for social discord and environmental disaster. People have started distrusting election results, not to mention the safety of the food they eat. What can be trusted? Access to information can and is being manipulated by, for example, Google's page-rank algorithm.

Blockchain technology is very much a manifestation or result of this erosion of trust. It has been proposed and is being developed to create a "trustless" system, one that doesn't require trust. This really is a new paradigm.

Blockchain enables decentralized peer-to-peer interactions of all types to take place within this system. You don't need to trust or even know the person on the other end of the transaction. However, you can rest assured that the transaction itself has been accurately recorded and not been tampered with. That's so powerful a step forward that it's transformative.

Let's stop pretending we haven't lost trust. Do we trust Facebook? Do we trust Google? Do we trust that the milk we buy at Whole Foods is safe: that the cows milked weren't abused; that the carton hasn't been sitting on the shelf for weeks; that the expiration date was marked correctly; and that it was properly refrigerated while it was shipped?

Probably, and in many cases certainly, not. The companies involved control and can manipulate any of this data. Just as importantly, people make mistakes and accidents happen. The wrong expiration date may be stamped on the carton of milk, not because some nefarious bad actor has consciously done so with evil intent, but because of an accounting error. Perhaps it's only an error, but data errors can have enormous consequences.

We've seen the tragic case of a commercial airliner's pitot tube malfunctioning and causing a mid-Atlantic crash. The crew may have assumed the plane was moving too slowly and perhaps coming to a stall, and corrected by dipping the nose down. The plane, however, wasn't in a stall or moving too slowly. The pitot tube simply wasn't reading the air velocity correctly. Taking over from autopilot, the human pilot had put the plane into a nose dive without even knowing it.

Similar catastrophes occur because the wrong anesthesia is administered in operating rooms. Or when some damned smart car notices "impending debris on the road" and stops randomly in the middle of a highway. Or because someone with a possibly fatal allergy has consumed a food that has not been properly marked. Again, all this is to say that "accounting errors," in the broadest sense, not only affect financial calculations, but can mean the difference between life and death.

Blockchain is an accounting tool, which hardly makes it sound sexy and cool. To try to make it seem sexy and cool would be bullsh*t. Unless we're talking about actuaries gone wild, but that's a different story. However, blockchain is also a really powerful accounting tool: a ledger that's also a distributed network on which data, once recorded, can't be changed.

As a reminder, the original ledgers were created to keep accounts of crops and were essential tools in launching the agricultural revolution. Blockchain technology has the potential to be just as revolutionary and transformative. Blockchain is a response to the distrust—the "trust gaps"—that globalization has brought about, and the technology is poised to shift how we transact, communicate, and organize.

What I've aimed to do in this book is broaden your perspective on blockchain and crypto—what the technologies are, why they are, and what their potential is—beyond the buzzwords and the bullsh*t. We're at such an early stage of this technology's development that almost anything that can be said about it is bound to be speculative and controversial. Everything I've said is my own perspective—the perspective of someone who's been involved with these technologies since before the beginning.

What has already happened is fascinating and exciting to me, and what's going to happen will be even more so. Yes, blockchain is an "accounting tool," which may make it seem dull, but for reasons I hope you now understand, it's a technology that energizes and excites me. It's not just a technology. It's a global paradigm shift that will impact the way we live and relate to and transact with one another.

What I urge you to do, above all, is get involved. Crypto and blockchain are still in the early, creative phase. Thinking through the new business and sociocultural models that blockchain enables is and will be as important as developing the underlying technology.

It's important to be deeply aware of the exponential pace at which everything is moving. To this end, I've created a website where you can find a list of resources and glossary of blockchain- and crypto-related terms, along with other fun tidbits. Check it out at BitcoinPizzabook.com.

This is something we can all do together. Please get in touch via the website if you or your team would like to learn more about evolving Web 3.0 trends, emerging technologies, and their implications, or if you'd like to work together on transformative business applications. If you've learned anything from what I've said, I hope you realize that blockchain is truly the operating system of the future—and the future is now.

Oh, right! I almost forgot about the Pizza. I told you there would be Pizza. Ready to get started with blockchain now?

Great!

LET THERE BE PIZZA!

(To scan: Take a photo of the QR code with your smartphone or use a QR code reader. Yum!)

Thanks for reading. See you back in the interwebs!

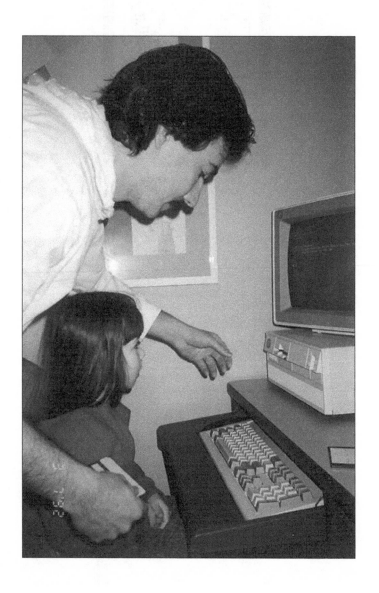

ACKNOWLEDGMENTS

I've always been a bit ahead of my time. "Three-going-on-thirty," they always said. Whether it was seeking to understand the atmosphere's chemical composition at age five, learning calculus to find the exact area of my ketchup bottle at age nine, or taking college classes in drama and social psychology at Oxford at age sixteen, I've always been seeking and looking ahead.

But it hasn't always been easy to see beyond conventional paradigms, beyond our present reality, beyond technology, or beyond myself.

To those who've helped me along this journey, those who've kept me grounded—even when I wanted so badly to fly planes, jump out of them, or let my imagination float off into la-la land—I owe it all to you.

To my parents, grandparents, siblings, extended family:

You raised me, you empowered me, you endured my incessant questioning and soulful pondering. You are what made me, me. Even when you asked if I came with an "off button."

To the radiant Sun in my life, Jacqueline York O'Neill, to whom we owe this book's *New Yorker*-worthy illustrations: I couldn't think of anyone I'd rather experience all this with. Forever your Moon.

To my friends: You know who you are. I'm so honored to be able to call all you creatives, artists, writers, actors, and entrepreneurs my buddies. We're the wacky, wild, and crazy ones, eh? Let's please form the 2020 version of the Bloomsbury Group.

To my mentors, teachers, professors, coaches: Thank you for helping me inhabit my presence, feel grateful in my bigness, and learn to overflow into and catalyze the world. Particularly, thank you for letting me write in a colloquial voice for academic papers, encouraging me to pursue my first startup instead of a PhD, then also taking it back and telling me I should have started a theater troupe rather than technology company, and letting me do crazy things like shoot documentaries instead of write. Look at me now!

To Tom Lane and the entire Scribe Media team: I wouldn't have written this without you, literally.

I am forever grateful for my friend, the talented artist and photographer Ashley Kolodner, who shot the wonderful photo used as my headshot as part of her award-winning project "Gayface." Follow her at @ashleykolodner and see more of her work at ashleykolodner.com.

To my team at Chronicled, teams at previous companies, teams that I have advised, invested in, consulted for, and crossed paths with: Thank you for expanding my knowledge and consciousness. Above all, thank you for giving so much of yourselves to a mission, and for learning and growing together along the way.

To all the amazing folks who come out to see my talks, invite me to speak, and welcome me with open arms when sharing my stories and ideas: You are why I do what I do. I never dreamed I could make a career out of this.

To all of the ladies and diverse folks out there hustling to go hard in business: I salute you. It's a hard, hard road, and you're all building it with each step you take.

To the ladies of The Collective Future: Satoshi IS female!

To all of the crypto community: Thank you for building, thinking, debating, changing how we see the world, and having a little fun along the way.

To Satoshi Nakamoto: Thank you, above all, for starting a much-needed conversation.

Life can sometimes seem like you've dumped a box of Ping-Pong balls into a tiny room and they're bouncing all over the place in a chaos of movement and noise, with no coherent order or linearity.

In hindsight, I can see that I am here, right now, exactly where I'm supposed to be. But it hasn't seemed that way all along. It didn't seem like it was part of the plan when I was kicked out of my first-grade class for hyperactivity, only to be sent to the theater to partake in the production of *The Wizard of Oz*—a play that's also a critique of the financial system—instead of class. Yet I now stand on stages, talking about blockchain and business, multiple times a month.

Our future seems a bit like that. We might not be able to see what's coming yet, and it might not take a linear path, but in time we'll get there.

We're all taking part in building a new social operating system, the operating system of the future. A better future. A future where we restore connections with ourselves, with each other, with our environment, and with the products we consume.

This is a unique moment in human history; there's no

doubt about it. We're experiencing seismic paradigm shifts on the sociocultural, geopolitical, financial, and environmental levels. Blockchain and, more broadly, decentralization are simply technical manifestations of these broader ideas. To me, they represent, at the very least, the continuation of Satoshi's much-needed conversation about the shifts from centralized to decentralized, from opaque to transparent, and from a culture of distrust to trust.

Let's move forward, boldly, into a better future by continuing a conversation that has only just begun.

Onwards!

Sam

ABOUT THE AUTHOR

SAMANTHA RADOCCHIA is an early blockchain pioneer and advocate who combines the mindsets of an anthropologist and a technologist. She's led corporate trainings at Fortune 100 companies, governments, and the United Nations, educating leaders on the technologies and cultural shifts that will shape their organizations—and daily lives—in the decades to come. Sam is a contributor to *Forbes* and was named to their 30 Under 30 list in 2017. A three-time entrepreneur, she holds several patents and is a co-founder of Chronicled, an enterprise blockchain company focused on supply chain. She now consults with executives on emerging technologies and delivers keynotes at events worldwide as she works to build her next company.

9 781544 504414